Holy Serpent
of the Jews

About the Cover of This Book

The *biscione* is an Italian heraldic charge showing a serpent in the act of consuming a child. Some claim that the child is coming *out* of the serpent's mouth and is the prophesied antichrist, son of Satan. The biscione was the emblem of the House of Visconti from the 11th century when that royal family controlled the city of Milan.

The word biscione is derived from the Italian *bistia* (Latin: *bestia*), in English—beast. As the symbol of Milan, the biscione is also used in a stylistic design as logo by the *Alfa Romeo* car manufacturer.

The biscione is often seen as wearing a crown on the head of the serpent. But on the cover of *Holy Serpent of the Jews,* the crown is *not shown* since only Jesus Christ is deserving of honor as King.

HOLY SERPENT
OF THE JEWS

The Rabbis' Secret Plan for Satan to
Crush Their Enemies and Vault
the Jews to Global Dominion

TEXE MARRS

RCP RiverCrest Publishing

1708 Patterson Road • Austin, Texas 78733

ACKNOWLEDGEMENTS

My staff deserves maximum praise for their outstanding contributions. Included: Michelle Powell, business administrator, Sandra Myers, publishing and art; Jerry Barrett, computer and internet; Nelson Sorto, shipping and facilities manager; and Steve Reilly, administration and shipping. To my wife and confidant, Wanda Marrs, goes all my love and gratefulness.

Holy Serpent of the Jews: The Rabbis' Secret Plan for Satan to Crush Their Enemies and Vault the Jews to Global Dominion

All Scripture quotations are from the King James Version of the Holy Bible

Cover design: Sandra Myers and Texe Marrs

Printed in the United States of America

Library of Congress Catalog Card Number 2016937240

Categories: 1. Judaism   2. Occult/New Age
               3. Religion   4. Political Science
               5. Current Events

ISBN 978-1-930004-98-6

"In that day the Lord
with his sore and great and strong sword
shall punish leviathan the piercing serpent,
even leviathan that crooked serpent; and he
shall slay the dragon that is in the sea."

—Isaiah 27:1

OTHER BOOKS BY TEXE MARRS

Churches and Pastors Gone Wild!: America's Christian Establishment Has Gone Berserk!

DNA Science and the Jewish Bloodline

Robot Alchemy: Androids, Cyborgs, and the Magic of Artificial Life

Conspiracy of the Six-Pointed Star: Eye-opening Revelations and Forbidden Knowledge About Israel, the Jews, Zionism, and the Rothschilds

Conspiracy World: A Truthteller's Compendium of Eye-Opening Revelations and Forbidden Knowledge

Mysterious Monuments: Encyclopedia of Secret Illuminati Designs, Masonic Architecture, and Occult Places

Codex Magica: Secret Signs, Mysterious Symbols and Hidden Codes of the Illuminati

Mystery Mark of the New Age: Satan's Design for World Domination

Days of Hunger, Days of Chaos

Project L.U.C.I.D.: The Beast 666 Universal Human Control System

Circle of Intrigue: The Hidden Inner Circle of the Global Illuminati Conspiracy

Dark Majesty: The Secret Brotherhood and the Magic of a Thousand Points of Light

Millennium: Peace, Promises, and the Day They Take Our Money Away

New Age Cults and Religions

Dark Secrets of the New Age

OTHER BOOKS BY RIVERCREST PUBLISHING

Matrix of Gog: From the Land of Magog Came the Khazars to Destroy and Plunder, *by Daniel Patrick*

Synagogue of Satan, *by Andrew Carrington Hitchcock*

New Age Lies to Women, *by Wanda Marrs*

Bohemian Grove: Cult of Conspiracy, *by Mike Hanson*

Behind Communism, *by Frank L. Britton*

FOR MORE INFORMATION

For a complete catalog of books, tapes, and videos about the Illuminati, secret societies, occultism, Bible prophecy, conspiracy and related topics, and for a free sample of Texe Marrs' informative newsletter, *Power of Prophecy*, please phone toll-free 1-800-234-9673, or write to: RiverCrest Publishing, 1708 Patterson Rd, Austin, Texas 78733. For additional information we highly recommend the following website:

www.powerofprophecy.com

TABLE OF Contents

The Jews: A Great People, a Priestly People on a Global Scale?

"We are being born as a great people, a priestly people on a global scale now."

—Michael Margolis
"Leviathan and the Great Purification"

S atan has a Plan for a One World Religion and a One World Government. This religion will be led by his chosen people, the Jews. The Holy Serpent, the beast whom the rabbis adore as Messiah, will rise up out of the abyss. He will anoint the Jews as gods and destroy their hated adversaries, the Christians.

This destruction shall be known as "The Great Purification." After the hated Christians are vanquished, the Jews, now divine gods of Planet Earth, will celebrate their victory at a momentous Feast of the Beast. This shall be a holy Eucharist at which they shall eat the flesh of the Holy Serpent. Thus, shall the Kingdom of the Jews be filled with Light and the age of the Jewish Utopia be inaugurated.

The above statement captures the true and accurate theological basis of today's Judaism. I will prove conclusively in this book that the rabbis teach these incredible things and that they are deeply ingrained in the

Judaic religion.

Frankly, I find that Judaism is a repugnant and loathsome religion. Judaism is a phallic sex cult based on self-worship by Jews and on the adoration of none other than the Serpent. Yes, that's right, the god, and messiah for the Jews is Satan, who is the serpent.

Worse, the Jews, who comprise only a tiny percentage of the world's population, are nevertheless in such powerful and influential positions today that they are capable of bringing their monstrous religious beliefs to reality. That belief system includes the conquest of America and the world by the Jewish elite and the establishment of a dictatorial New World Order.

These facts are so astounding, so mind-boggling that I feel obligated to explain.

The Conventional Wisdom is Wrong

Three decades ago, in 1987, my book, *Dark Secrets of the New Age*, was published. It became an instant bestseller, rising to the top of the Christian Bestsellers List. In that book, I warned of the unexpected emergence of a vast planetary network of *thousands* of *networking* New Age cults, religious, and spiritual entities. In a follow up book, *New Age Cults and Religions*, I examined over 100 of these extraordinary groups, and I included in the book a chart, contrasting the 12 principal beliefs, or doctrines, of the New Age with the doctrines of Bible Christianity.

Neither book focused on the supposed monotheistic religion of Judaism.

At the time of their writing I knew little about Judaism and its essential doctrines. Raised an evangelical, like almost every other Christian I erroneously believed that Christianity was simply an extension—even the *completion*—of Judaism, the religion of the Jews.

Christian Pastors and theologians again and again reassured me and other Christians that Jews believed only in the *Old Testament*. Christianity and its *New Testament* added the story of Jesus and the Cross to Judaism. To understand Judaism, these Pastors say, all one has to do is read and study the Old Testament. The Christian Pastors and teachers had even coined and frequently used the term, *Judeo-Christianity* when referring to the religion of Jesus Christ and to the Western culture. I, too, believed in "Judeo-Christianity."

It therefore appeared the case that the New Age movement and its numerous cults and religions were being built and quickly expanded across the globe in *opposition* to Judeo-Christianity. I surmised, therefore, that the rabbis must be allied with Christian pastors and teachers in this holy war against Judeo-Christianity.

My family, church, and community further fostered and supported my belief in Judeo-Christianity. My elderly mother had always assured me that the Jews were "God's Chosen."

My father told me the Jews were the "Apple of God's eye." The evangelical Pastors glowingly told their congregations of the blessings we Christians would receive if we blessed the Jews. After all, they said, the Jews are the very "Seed of Abraham."

Lies of the Rabbis

None of these things are true.

The Pastors had simply neglected to read and study the Bible. They simply accepted the smooth and deceptive lies of the rabbis. My parents, too, were incorrect. They unfortunately believed the Pastors and passed on the "conventional wisdom."

These lies of the rabbis originated centuries ago, but caught on inside the Church no more than 125 years ago. The corrupt scoundrel, Cyrus Scofield, worked with wealthy Jews in New York and even published a new Bible with their money and assistance. You can read about this criminal con-man, Cyrus Scofield, in the excellent book, *The Incredible Scofield and His Book.*

None of the founding fathers of the Church—from Jesus and the Apostles, all the way to Luther and Tyndale—believed in these things. Truly, Satan has been a great success at poisoning the minds of Christians in recent decades, causing many to accept the strange concepts of Judaic superiority, physical Israel, and the Old Covenant.

Subsequently, I went through a 20-year career in the U.S. Air Force, retiring in 1982 as an officer and having commanded a number of successful units. I was also blessed to have graduated *summa cum laude* with a Bachelors Degree in Political Science

Cyrus I. Scofield was a crook and con-man who abandoned his wife and fled Kansas. He showed up in New York City where he joined the exclusive Lotus Club. Wealthy Jews helped him to publish his own edition of the Bible, the Scofield Bible. The notes in his Bible were pro-Zionist and spurred the Judaizer movement in evangelical churches. Today, evangelicals, especially Baptists, revere Scofield as a saint.

and a Master's Degree from North Carolina State University. I then taught for five years on the full-time faculty of the prestigious University of Texas at Austin and upon retirement, founded Tech Trends, a high-tech consulting business. I authored a dozen books on practical technology and other topics.

Then, in 1986, my wife, Wanda and I gave our lives fully to Jesus Christ. That made all the difference in the world. I opened the pages of my Holy Bible and immediately set upon a great spiritual odyssey studying false cults and religions and focusing on the burgeoning, fast growth of the New Age movement.

That is when I wrote and published *Dark Secrets of the New Age, New Age Cults and Religions,* and other works. I became celebrated in Christendom for these titles and was eventually recognized as possibly the world's foremost authority on cults and satanic religions. Still, I was not in the least conversant about Judaism—the real Judaism.

I Studied the Kabbalah

In studying the New Age movement, I continually came across a series of books related to the *Kabbalah*. These books were prominently displayed on the shelves of New Age bookstores. I bought most of the books on *Kabbalah* and quickly realized that they were part and parcel of the New Age. I also discovered that the *Kabbalah* was extremely important to *Judaism*.

Moreover, I learned that Judaism has little to do with the Old Testament. Rabbinical Seminaries—called *Yeshivas*—pay little or no attention to the Old Testament. The majority of their studies have to do with the *Babylonian Talmud*, the Jews' books (actually some 68 volumes) of 613 laws and commentaries.

In the Talmud are many teachings of the Kabbalah. And most rabbis combine both the Talmud and the Kabbalah to round out their Jewish theological education.

This means, of course, that Judaism, infused with teachings of the Kabbalah and the Talmud, is New Age to its very core.

Given this inescapable connection, I have now spent almost 30 years studying both the Talmud and the Kabbalah, contrasting these foundational books of Judaism with the doctrines and beliefs of New Age cults and religions. Here are the facts regarding my research:

- Judaism is a rabbinical cult. It is not based on revelation but on a combination of skewed human reason and rampant human fantasy. Both the Talmud and the Kabbalah are authored by

Yeshiva students in Israel. Future rabbis study the Talmud and Kabbalah. Most spend no time at all directly studying the Torah, the first books of the Old Testament. They are taught that the Talmud is more holy and more worthy of study.

biased Jewish rabbis who have rejected the truth of Jesus Christ.

- While the Talmud does have 613 laws and the Jew must attempt to navigate through all of these very petty and often silly rules, Judaism is not centered on the rigid Talmud but, instead, on the imaginative and fantastical books of the Kabbalah.

- The Kabbalah is at the very heart of Judaism. It grips the religious Jew with it's bizarre doctrinal structure and introduces a fascinating array of mystical, magical practices to occupy his mind and his energy.

- These mystical, magical practices of the Kabbalah include gematria (the magic of numerology), astrology, necromancy (communicating with dead spirits), color mysticism, chanting, mantras, dream interpretation, astral travel, goddess worship, sexual tantra, occult visualization, divination, occult symbolism, altered states of consciousness, psychic mind powers, idol worship, and other elements of witchcraft.

- The Kabbalah is derived from the Mystery Religions of Babylon, Persia, Sumeria, Egypt, Greece, Rome, and other pagan cultures. The rabbis simply borrowed from these ancient writings. This is the reason for its similarity to other New Age cults and religions, which are also based on Mystery Teachings.

- Both the Talmud and the Kabbalah are racist documents. Both hold the conscious Jew as the ultimate in evolution and as gods on earth. Gentiles are but cattle and the Jews, as sparks of God, are destined to rule.

- The Kabbalah greatly expands the Talmud's concept of "God." The Kabbalah teaches of many minor gods and goddesses, including ten emanations of the unknowable, unapproachable supreme "God." Moreover, "God" has a wife, a Holy Presence known as "Shekinah."

- The Kabbalah is essentially a lewd guide for a mind-sick sex cult. One of the deities in the Kabbalah's Tree of Life is Yesod, the phallus! Yesod continually lusts after and has sex frequently with Malkuth, a goddess. Plus, a higher feminine deity, the goddess Binah, has sex with yet another god, Tiphereth. Satan, meanwhile, enjoys sex with both Binah and Malkuth, and with lesser personages of the multifaceted Jewish godhead. Meanwhile, Jewish persons here on earth copulate believing they are fostering frequent sex in the heavenlies by the gods and goddesses. *Judaism is a weird, lustful religion complete with human-god swingers and wild and frequent sex!* Even incestuous relations are encouraged among the gods and goddesses.

- The Kabbalah teaches that God encloses the universe within himself, that the Holy Serpent, named *Leviathan*, is the *"Angel of help"* that shall lift the Jew to rulership on Planet Earth, and that Jews must do both evil and good works to ascend to godhood. God, then, is Himself *both* good and evil, a combination of both the darkness and light.
- The Kabbalah teaches that the Holy Serpent is the Messiah of the Jews and the Great Secret is that the Serpent, is, in fact, the "God" of the Jews. As such, he is depicted as enclosing the entire universe inside himself as the Ouroboros, the eternal Serpent biting its own tail.

Satan's World Religion

These are the primary things you must know of the Talmud and the Kabbalah. You should be aware of these basic facts to be able to defend yourself, your family, and your nation in the ongoing war with Satan's World Religion. There are other things we will cover in this book, such as Judaism's embrace of the number of the Beast, 666. You will read also of *Tikkun Olam*, the Jewish Plan for a New World Order and of the Great Purification mentioned in their Kabbalah.

Michael Margolis, a Jew and an authority on the Kabbalah, suggests that humanity is now at the threshold of the coming of Leviathan, the Serpent. The Great Purification is at hand. He says of the Jews, *"We are being born as a great people, a priestly people on a global scale now."*

Many other rabbis echo Mr. Margolis, trumpeting the claim that the Serpent is about to complete his long journey and that the New Age Kingdom of the Jews, their Utopia, is ready to be unveiled.

In the pages of this book, we carefully examine Mr. Margolis' thesis and that of other rabbinical authorities. Their ideas and doctrines, of course, are diametrically opposite of the truths expressed so long ago by our Lord and Saviour, Jesus Christ. He exposed the Judaic religion as a destroyer religion based on *"man-made traditions."* He told the religious Jews that they were of their father, the devil; and he warned the Jews that the Kingdom is taken away from them and given to another nation that will have faith in Him (Matthew 21:53).

Peter, the Apostle of Jesus, likewise believed his Messiah, Jesus. In *I Peter 2:9* he gave the world the truth about the Jews who claim to be a "priestly people on a global scale." But Peter said of Christians: "...ye are a chosen people, a royal priesthood, an holy nation, a peculiar people that ye should shew forth the praises of Him who hath called you out of darkness into his marvelous light."

Judaism, having rejected the words of Christ and of Peter, his disciple, stubbornly clings to its racist dogma that only the Jews are a great and priestly people. The New Testament concludes otherwise. It proclaims that Jesus Christ has chosen His people out of all the nations and races on earth. Jews, Gentiles—it makes no difference to Jesus: *"Whosoever will may come."*

My prayer is that all who read this book will believe in the saving words of Jesus Christ, and come to the Cross of Calvary.

ONE

Do the Jews Live Within the Belly of the Holy Serpent? Is He the Deity Whom the Jews Worship?

The Holy Serpent of the Jews

"Ye serpents, ye generation (race or nation) of vipers, how can ye escape the damnation of hell?"
— Jesus Christ
Matthew 23:33

If I were to tell you that in the religion of Judaism the deity worshipped is the *Holy Serpent*, would you believe me? Few people would. Yet, it is absolutely true! In Judaism the deity most honored and venerated is, in fact, the Holy Serpent.

Now don't let the name Texe Marrs get in your way of discovering this awful truth. Some might contend that Texe Marrs is, after all, an anti-Semite, and an anti-Semite cannot be believed, right?

Let's say, then, that we ask the rabbis themselves, the top rabbis in the world. We could even go to the writings of the rabbinical sages—to some of the most famous rabbis who ever lived, so-called "holy men" whose historical writings to this day are frequently quoted and referred to as authoritative and definitive in the study of Judaic doctrine.

The Serpent Shall Rise From the Abyss

Take, for example, the celebrated rabbi known throughout the Jewish religious world as the "Gaon of Vilna." It was he who taught of the

Kabbalah's doctrine that inside Judaism's vaunted Tree of Life there resides a great and Sacred Serpent whose masculine name is Leviathan and whose feminine name is Malkuth. It is this Sacred Serpent, the Kabbalah teaches, that in the coming Messianic age shall rise from the abyss to conquer the Gentiles and exalt God's Chosen, the Jews. This Leviathan, the holy and piercing serpent, is the expected Messiah prophesied to appear, the one who will supernaturally possess the bodies of the world's Jews and lead them to global domination and glory.

This strange doctrine, accepted by the vast majority of today's Orthodox Rabbis, also makes the bold claim that the Jews are a Holy Race of wise and virtuous *serpent beings*. Collectively, World Jewry *is* claimed to be the very incarnation on earth of the Holy Serpent.

Could this be what the true Messiah and Lord of the Universe, Jesus Christ, meant when he confronted the wicked pharisaic Jews—equivalent to today's Orthodox Jewry—by flatly declaring:

> *"Ye serpents, ye generation of vipers, how can ye escape the damnation of hell?" (Matthew 23:33)*

The House of Israel Left Desolate

In the King James Bible lexicon, the word *"generation"* here means "race, nation, bloodline, or ethnic group."

In this same Gospel, in *Matthew 23* we also find Jesus telling the Jews, *"Behold, your house is left unto you desolate."*

"Desolate!" That means devoid of spiritual value, barren, a wasteland. Today, the House of Israel, the physical nation of Israel, is exactly what Jesus said it would be—a spiritual desert, a nation of lying, deceiving, terrorist killers; desolate of morality, devoid of righteousness. All of Rothschild's trillions and all of America's boatloads of foreign aid, diplomatic cover, and military armaments heaped on the artificially created nation of Israel for the past six decades cannot change one iota of what Jesus prophesied. Israel is a desolate place, a wasteland of inhuman cruelty and savage conduct, and it shall remain so.

Moreover, except for a tiny remnant, the Jewish people, wherever they may reside, spiritually are "serpents"—serpents whose cruel, black hearts are stained with filth and contamination. Just so, because the priesthood of rabbis, the keepers of the Judaic faith, are worshippers of the Holy Serpent.

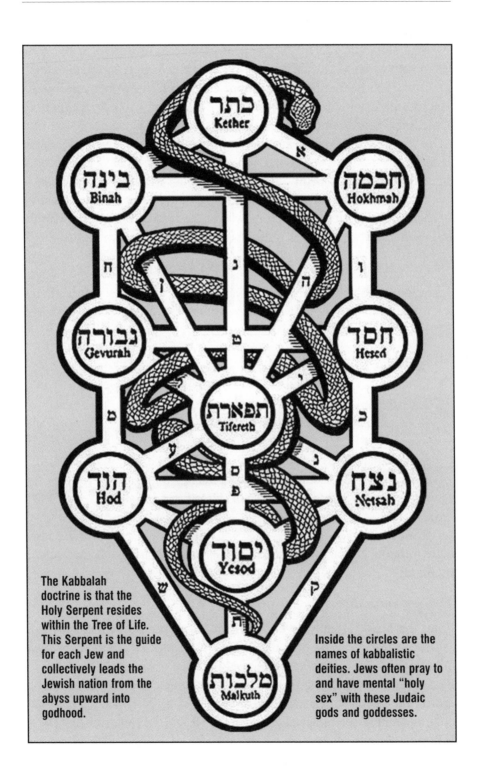

The Kabbalah doctrine is that the Holy Serpent resides within the Tree of Life. This Serpent is the guide for each Jew and collectively leads the Jewish nation from the abyss upward into godhood.

Inside the circles are the names of kabbalistic deities. Jews often pray to and have mental "holy sex" with these Judaic gods and goddesses.

The Holy (or Sacred) Serpent, of course, is identified in the New Testament as he who was cast out of heaven. In other words, the Devil, or Satan. The Sacred Serpent is represented in Hebrew gematria by the Hebrew alphabet letter "vav" of YHWH, the Jews' kabbalistic name for God. Since the Torah (the first five books of the Old Testament) are said to be "the heart of Jewish existence," the doctrine that the Sacred Serpent is hidden within the Torah and appears as the letter vav is an essential foundation of Judaic tradition. The rabbis believe that this letter—vav— is evidence of their deity. They emphasize that the letter vav, indicative of the Sacred Serpent, is found exactly at the middle-point of the Torah, at *Leviticus 11:42*, which is said to be the belly of the Serpent deity.

We Jews Have Landed in the Belly of the Serpent

Jerusalem scholar and rabbi, Joel David Bakst, excitedly writes of this doctrine which places the Jewish tribe within the very belly of the Sacred Serpent, exclaiming:

> "We have journeyed to the center of the world and landed in the belly of a serpent!" ("Journey to the Center of the Torah," *cityofluz.com*; also see the book, *The Secret Doctrine of the Gaon of Vilna Volume II*, by Joel David Bakst)

In the Zohar, the essential book of Jewish cabalistic magic, we find another amazing Judaism doctrinal statement: "The Holy Serpent is the fountainhead, root and essence for all of God's sacred, revelatory light..."

Read the above and ponder. Do you not see why Jesus told the Jews their religion is *not* of Abraham and is instead based on "man-made traditions?"

The Serpent is Satan and He is Not Holy!

From the New Testament we know that the serpent is neither holy nor sacred. Instead, he is described as *"that old serpent, called the Devil and Satan, which deceiveth the whole world" (Revelation 12:9)*.

However, in Judaism, as in all satanic religions, truth is turned upside down. The rabbis emphasize that the serpent is a godly being, a constant help and guide for Israel and its people. Rabbi Laitman, in his Daily Kabbalah Lesson of the Zohar, stresses that:

"...This snake comes as medication...an angel sent to us...we should be grateful to the serpent for its help...the serpent has a very important mission...

"The Serpent is the Angel of Help."

The deep secret of Judaism is the rabbis' teaching that the Jewish people—also known as the House of Israel—is within the Sacred Serpent's belly and that the Serpent is sent to the Jews to be their helpmate and guide. That is what is meant when Rabbi Moshel Rabbinu says that the religious Jew embarks on a spiritual "Journey to the Center of the Torah: The Secret in the Serpent's Belly" (see Joel David Bakst, 2007, *www.chazonhatorah.org*).

In Judaism's gematria, the so-called science of numbers, we find the teaching that the one whom Christians know as Satan, the Devil, is for the Jews the divine instrument of... "sacred, revelatory light... This serpent is...the middle brain which is in the middle of the letters of the Torah."

The rabbis further insist that it is their Holy Serpent, their deity, who is at the very center of the Torah. He is an essential being of their godhead, and he provides the serpentine energy that brings a Jew to a spiritually mature state. The religious Jew, say the rabbis, is brought to spiritual maturity—to a "Divine Consciousness"—through the help of the snake. He—that is, every Jew—lives *inside* the belly of the Serpent. He is their covering, protector, guide, Lord, and Messiah.

The rabbis go so far as to say that, "in messianic times and beyond, it (the Serpent) will be redeemed and revealed in all its glory and awesomeness." (Rabbi Joel David Bakst, "Journey to the Center of the Torah: The Secret in the Serpent's Belly," 2007, see also *www.cityofluz.com*)

Now do you see why God's Word twice in the book of *Revelation (Chapter 2:9 and 3:9)* warns of the horror and wickedness of the *"Synagogue of Satan?"*

The Serpent Guides the Jews to Redemption

According to the highest-ranking kabbalistic rabbis, the Serpent represents not only a specific deity, Lucifer, but also the whole nation, or people, of Israel. The House of Israel, collective of all the Jews wherever they may reside on this planet, is said to be the body of the Serpent. The head is claimed to be the Illuminati initiates who, behind the scenes, are masterminding and guiding the Serpent in his path of Redemption and global domination.

It is not simply that the most fanatical and zealous high priests of Judaism worship the divine Serpent; in the teachings of the Kabbalah, the Jewish People *are* the *"Serpent."* As such, as explained in the *Encyclopedia Judaica*, the Jewish People, as a whole are their own *"Messiah."* Every Jew is divine while all other people (the *Goyim*, or Gentiles) are less than human and are privileged to even be alive. Indeed, the *Goyim*, the Talmud emphasizes, are beasts fit only to be servants and slaves of Jewish *effendi* (masters).

The Serpent in the Talmud

The Talmud, the sacred law book of Judaism, includes a provision that on the Sabbath, one *"is permitted to charm snakes and serpents"* *(Sanhedrin 101a, 101b).*

To "charm" means to invoke, to invite or welcome, an entity (serpent or spirit) to come under your command and do your bidding. In this way, the beguiled snake could be induced by the charmer to stealthily seek out and destroy an enemy. The Zionist Serpent of Death, it is claimed, symbolically strikes at one enemy after another until all the world is bitten and defeated.

But the Serpent, in Judaic lore, legend and sectarian doctrine, is more than a servant of the Jews. He is the Spiritual Director of the Great Work of the Illuminati Jews, and from the beginning, he brought to this planet his alchemical powers of deceit and seduction. In this capacity the Serpent first met humankind, leading to his dialogue with Eve in the Garden of Eden, during which he questioned what God had told Adam and Eve: *"Surely, hath God said...?"*

In the theology of the kabbalists, we find Eve being praised as Mother and giver of divine knowledge. That she bit into the forbidden fruit (some say *apple*, most Jews say *pomegranate*) was a splendid thing as it resulted in divine status and inheritance for the Jews.

Throughout the Judaic faith we find the Holy Serpent venerated and worshipped by the Jews. In cemeteries one often finds the Serpent symbolized, indicating that the departed was one of the "Righteous." The Talmud *(Beza Meziah 84b, 85a)* teaches that serpents encircle the

Righteous during their lives, attending to their needs and guiding their actions. It is said by the rabbis that the Holy Serpent is the protector of Jews and their sacred covering.

The famous rabbi, Ibn Ezra, taught in the Talmud that, "Serpents stand as servants to do your will." The serpents represent various astral deities, stars, and planets, including Draco, the dragon and serpent constellation.

How very different is Christianity, in which it is emphasized that the serpent is cunning, subtle, a liar and murderer. He is, in fact, the very symbol of Satan himself.

Why This is Important

Many unwary and undiscerning people over the years have contacted me and asked, "Texe, why do you write and speak so much about the Jews, Israel, Zionism, and Judaism. Why is this subject so important?"

Frankly, it is because my Lord and Saviour, Jesus Christ, bids me do so. He Himself warned of the House of Israel, of its "abominations" and "desolation." He described it as the "Synagogue of Satan." Without flinching, He also identified the hateful and rebellious Jews as "serpents" and "vipers."

The Jews themselves, in their devilish religion of Judaism, *admit* their god is the Serpent. Their leaders well know that this is the Devil, or Satan. In some type of creepy and eerie doctrinal confession, the rabbis are even discovered to be boasting of their Holy Serpent and they say that all Jews live inside its belly! Is this not unbelievable and revelatory?

Nevertheless, even the Jew can be saved. The Old Testament prophet *Isaiah (chapter 59)* testified that, indeed, the nation of Israel is of the Serpent. But the prophet also spoke of God's mercy and willingness to save those who repent of this evil.

"Behold, the Lord's hand is not shortened, that it cannot save; neither His ear heavy that it cannot hear:

"But your iniquities have separated between you and your God, and your sins have hid his His face from you, that He will not hear.

"For your hands are defiled with blood, and your fingers with iniquity; your lips have spoken lies, your tongue has muttered perverseness...

"They hatch cockatrice' (flying serpent) eggs, and weave the spider's web: he that eateth of their eggs dieth, and that which is crushed breaketh out into a viper."

TWO

The Jews have Destroyed Every Nation in Which They Gained Power... What Must Be Done Now to Preserve America From This Pitiful Fate?

Jaws of the Serpent

"We Jews, we the destroyers, will remain the destroyers forever. Nothing that you do will meet our needs and demands. We will forever destroy, because we need a world of our own, a God-World, which it is not in your nature to build."

> — Maurice Samuel
> *You Gentiles* (p. 155)

"Ye serpent, ye generation (race or nation) of vipers, how can ye escape the damnation of hell?"
> — *Matthew 23:3*

America is in dire jeopardy for we find ourselves now gripped tightly in the jaws of the serpent. To explain to you the seriousness of our current terrible dilemma, I declare to you the three *key truths* you and I must acknowledge if we are to save ourselves, our loved ones, and our nation:

1. Truth—The Jews and the Jewish Nation are in *bondage* to and

are under the control of their god. Their god is, without question, Satan, the Devil and Serpent of Perdition.

2. Truth—The Jews, like termites from hell, have undermined and eventually have *destroyed every nation* in which they resided and acquired dominance.

3. Truth—The Jews have now gained the upper-hand in American politics and culture, and our nation is now suffering the painful, parasite-infested process of unholy destruction.

The history of Great Britain, Germany, Russia, Poland, the former Soviet republics and satellites, and now the United States, demonstrates that what I declare here is true. Never have the Jews as a people peaceably assimilated. Inevitably, they remain a separate Jewish Nation, a People of the Holy Serpent, alien and foreign to the nation in which they reside. And wherever they exist, the Jews' devilish religion, toxin-producing culture, and hatred of other races and nationalities drives them to act as *Destroyers*.

The Destroyers

Slowly, inexorably, the Jewish minority in America has, through stealth, deceit, cunning, and treachery, burrowed like parasitic termites into the muscle and sinew of society. Their lobby and pressure groups—the Anti-Defamation League (ADL), the American Civil Liberties Union (ACLU), the Southern Poverty Law Center (SPLC), the American Jewish Committee (AJC), and many others—have bought, bribed, threatened or otherwise manipulated our Congress. The presidency also is now under their bulging influence.

Our entertainment industry is thoroughly Jewish and sickeningly satanic; our media is controlled by the Jewish elite and used as a weapon to destroy the patriotic opposition. The Zionist-controlled judiciary spits on our constitution and makes a mockery of our traditions. The education establishment is now under the Jewish thumb, and our universities and public schools have become satanic mills, disparaging America's once illustrious history, desecrating our nation's Gentile founders by branding them "dead white men," and ridiculing and denigrating our Bill of Rights and our Constitution.

Even America's health system is being ravaged. Socialist principles— the Jewish Death Machine—are now to be implemented in hospitals,

An ad for "Crown Royal" whiskey, by Seagram's. Seagram's Distillery, the world's largest whiskey corporation, is owned by the wealthy Bronfman family. The late Edgar Bronfman was head of the World Jewish Congress.

medical clinics, and in doctors' offices.

The Big Brother Police State has become a work of Luciferian art as Israeli "advisors" are called upon and paid billions of taxpayer dollars to set up new high tech systems of surveillance and control. The evidence points to actual Gulag concentration camps built and readied, in which we who dare to oppose this radical, Leninist transformation of society will be herded like cattle into pens. After all, the Jews' holy book, the Talmud, counts us as the *Goyim*, cattle fit only for blood and slaughter.

Our Ruling Gods

The Jewish minority in America has become our ruling "gods." This is nothing less than an extension of 18th, 19th and 20th century Illuminism,

Bolshevism and Communism. The Jews among us have become the *Dictatorship of the Proletariat,* and the *Vanguard of the Revolution,* as the savage Jew, Lenin, and his butcher associates called it.

"Classicism" has become the reigning ideology in America, and there are just two classes: Them and Us.

They have 545 puppets to assist them in their hellish Great Work—which is the causing of *Chaos* (*Ordo Ab Chao* is their Masonic/Jewish motto). This 545 consists of 535 (House and Senate), nine Supreme Court justices, and one president. That means 545 vs over 300 million citizens.

However, the 545 are like "Demon Pretzels," they wind, they bend, they twist according to the demands of their behind-the-scenes Jewish Masters. And increasingly, the nefarious work of the Jews is no longer done "behind-the-scenes." So successful are they in their takeover of America that they now dare—nay, gloat—to "go public" and to wallow in their dominance and superiority.

Thus we have the Schumers, the Liebermans, the Kerrys and all the other Jewish politicians leading a Communist/Zionist revolution in the Congress. Meanwhile, Jewish billionaires in Chicago actually crow and sound off in such controlled publications as *The Chicago Tribune* and other elitist news media, openly revealing that, *"Obama is America's first Jewish President"* (see documentation in my video, *Rothschild's Choice*).

Financial Tyranny and Economic Destruction

The plot of the Wall Street Jews and their collaborators is financial tyranny and economic destruction. The Jews who run the Federal Reserve, the Securities and Exchange Commission, the FDIC, the Treasury Department, and, of course, all the globalist money control groups (IMF, World Bank, International Bank of Settlements, etc.) are now leveling America. They are busily outsourcing America's industry and jobs, and otherwise fracturing and decimating our livelihoods.

America is slated to become the pitiful, knee-bowing servant to Red China and its dragon-loving dictators. And as I prove in *Conspiracy of the Six-Pointed Star,* it is Zionist Jews who first used their peasant servant, Mao Tse Tung, to conquer China and set up its murderous bureaucracy.

The End of Nationalism

The authoritarian Communist nation beloved of the Jewish elite is replacing America in the New World Order hierarchy of nations. In fact, America is under rapid dissolution as an independent nation with a cohesive people. The Jews are responsible for the 50 million Mexicans, Asians, Moslems, and other illegals that have invaded and flooded our country. Their *Protocols of Zion* calls for an end to national sovereignty. They seek to destroy our Christian traditions by immersing America into a cesspool of foreign cultism and alien religious philosophies.

We are given no choice in this matter as they force on us what they euphemistically call *"creative destruction."* Whether we elect Democrats or Republicans, left-wingers or rightists, the result is the same. American politics is now the preserve of an un-elected elite. They have formed a *Soviet Politburo* in Washington, D.C. and its dictatorial membership acts as would a *Sanhedrin*.

Zionist psychopaths and aliens, accompanied by lackey Gentile opportunists, have taken the reins and are plunging America into a black hole.

The Serpent Within the Serpent

Recently I had the "pleasure" (if you can call it that) of studying an essay written by a so-called "learned" American rabbi. It was entitled, *"The Serpent Within the Serpent."* In it, the rabbi openly and enthusiastically admitted that the religion of the Jews is based on worship of the Holy Serpent. Moreover, he noted that in the Kabbalah, the occult philosophy so in vogue in Israel and among today's Jewish community, the world's *Jewish Nation* not only venerates and adores this Serpent Deity, but is itself divine. The Jews, collectively are the divine *"Serpent Within the Serpent."*

And so it is that America is in its death throes. We are held as in a tight and constricting vise in the jaws of the most poisonous of Serpents, an aggressive viper more deadly and lethal than the feared King Cobra or Black Mamba. There is a preponderance of evidence that what I say about our current predicament is true.

What Are We Going to Do?

The question we must now answer if America and we are to survive as a free nation is, what are we going to do about it? We must act, and soon, or the jaws of the Serpent will tighten further and crush us into oblivion.

My writing and publishing *Conspiracy of the Six-Pointed Star* and this current title, *Holy Serpent of the Jews,* is my own small contribution to accomplishing the great task that lies before us. More such works will follow, God willing.

Do you, as do I, yearn to breathe free? Are you brave enough and willing to do what is necessary to constitutionally overthrow those who oppress us? Remember, Jews are the minority, even though they have in the palms of their greedy hands the outlaw 545 in Washington, D.C.

Whatever we do, we must make sure that we are in God's Will. We must follow His lead, or else we shall find ultimate victory outside our grasp. But if we obey God, and if, under His guidance, we employ the weapons of faith and perseverance, we will prevail. We can and will rise up and defeat this ruling elite—the tyrannical and alien Jewish minority and their disgusting, renegade puppets, the 545.

That is our struggle, not to simply escape from the jaws of the Serpent, but to deal that Serpent from hell a final death blow. It was the great reformer Martin Luther who nailed his 95 Theses to the door of the Wittenberg Chapel, declaring *"Here I stand."* What a wonderfully inspiring anthem are those three all-powerful words: "Here I stand." Tell me, dear reader, where, yes where, do *you* stand?

THREE

The Great Symbol of Solomon and It's Serpent

"But there is a God in heaven that revealeth secrets, and maketh known...what shall be in the latter days."
— *Daniel 2:28*

In the mid 1800s, Alphonse Louis Constant, a Jesuit priest who wrote under the Jewish pseudonym, Eliphas Levi, published his infamous work, *The Mysteries of Magic*. Levi was an ardent student of the Jewish Kabbalah and he discovered in it the keys to many occult mysteries. Chief among these mysteries is what is revealed on the *Great Symbol of Solomon*.

Solomon, though a wise man, in his old age became entrapped in the occult world by virtue of his many foreign wives and concubines. As a result, the great King of Israel brought the idols of Ashtoreth into the Temple and worshipped false gods such as Milcom (or Moloch). His arcane knowledge is seen in *I Kings 10:14* where we discover that Solomon annually required of the High Priests of the Temple a tribute, consisting of exactly 666 pieces of gold.

At base level, the worship of Ashtoreth and Milcom was the veneration of the Serpent. Thus, the Great Symbol of Solomon depicts the Holy Serpent as the Ouroboros, the eternal snake in a circle biting its own tail. Indeed, the Ouroboros serpent encompasses the whole of nature and existence and he is wrapped around the macroprosopus and the microprosopus, that is the god of light and the god of darkness. In both the upper, paradise world and in the abyss, below, we find the sexual symbols of *regeneration,* and we see also the two triangles joined together and becoming the sexually charged six-pointed star (called the Star of David).

As Above, So Below

This is also a symbol of Kabbalah and reflects both mercy and vengeance, and the concept, *As Above, So Below.* As Above, So Below is a magical principle that what happens in the spiritual world is reflected in the physical world.

Thus, Jehovah has two sides, good and evil, light and dark. Jehovah is said to be a Janus-like deity. Ultimately, Satan, or the devil, and God are simply the flip side of each other.

The kabbalist believes that Satan is the Holy Serpent, but he is also a *reflection* of the unknowable, ineffable and mysterious creator-god. The Creator-God, called by the Kabbalist *Ein Sof,* sends sparks of light out into the world. Satan is a reflector of this light. He is called by occultists the *Father of Light.*

The kabbalistic doctrine holds that the exalted race man, exclusively the Jew, honors the Holy Serpent as god. Not just any god, but a great and fearsome god. In the Kabbalah, we discover that Leviathan is the Holy Serpent. Leviathan is described in the Bible in the book of *Isaiah 27:1:*

> *"In that day the LORD with his sore and great and strong sword shall punish leviathan the piercing serpent, even leviathan that crooked serpent; and he shall slay the dragon that is in the sea."*

Leviathan is called the *"crooked serpent"* and the *"piercing serpent."* Crooked, or corrupt, we understand, but why the *piercing* serpent? Apparently, this is a Jewish allusion to Jesus Christ, who was pierced and afflicted on the cross. As was prophesied in *Zechariah,* we read, *"They shall look upon me whom they have pierced and they shall mourn, as one mourneth for his only son..."*

So pleased were the Jews with this description in *Isaiah* of Leviathan as the "crooked and piercing" serpent that in their kabbalistic doctrine the rabbis actually made the Holy Serpent their *Redeemer* and *Messiah. Thus, the Holy Serpent is the* opposite, or reverse, of Jesus.

In this way, Jesus is degraded and his reputation sullied and darkened. He is an evil being in the Talmud and Kabbalah. But his opposite side,

This ancient occult Seal of Solomon depicts the Holy Serpent (the Oroboros) encircling the Jewish Man and six-pointed star in an As Above, So Below pattern.

Satan, the Holy Serpent, is depicted as righteous and good.

Satan Glorified

Such specious and monstrous reasoning is often found in the pages of the Kabbalah and Talmud. In the Kabbalah, the devil is not described as the "Old Dragon and Satan." Nor is he termed the "Fallen Angel." Instead, we read in Jewess Helena Blavatsky's *The Secret Doctrine* that, "The most learned, if not the greatest of modern kabbalists, namely Eliphas Levi, describes Satan in the following glowing terms:

> "It is that Angel who was proud enough to believe himself God, brave enough to buy his independence at the price of eternal suffering and torture, beautiful enough to have adorned himself in full divine light; strong enough to reign in darkness amidst agony, and to have built himself a throne on his inextinguishable pyre. It is Satan, the prince of anarchy, served by a hierarchy of pure spirits" (*History of Magic*, pp. 16-17).

This Satan, writes Blavatsky, is the Angel of Self-sacrifice, who symbolizes the intellectual independence of conscious humanity. He is an "ever active energy," the *Force* of the generative power of sexual man. He has, said Blavatsky, been finally transformed into a Serpent—the Red Dragon, and made anthropomorphic.

Blavatsky confesses that, *"This devil was mankind, and never had any existence outside of that mankind."* This assertion is the key to understanding the Jewish Holy Serpent. As we shall see, in the Kabbalah and in Judaism, the cunning and subtle Holy Serpent, as Holy Redeemer and Messiah, guides and teaches the individual Jew on his or her journey along the Tree of Life. The Jew rides the Serpent as he sinks downward into the dark abyss, then continues to ride the Serpent as it emerges out of the abyss upward into the light.

Finally, the Holy Serpent completes his revolution, he grasps onto and grabs his own tail. The exalted Jew, given more and more light through both good and bad Mitzvahs (works), attains self-godhood. He no longer needs the Holy Serpent. He is the Holy Serpent, and he is thus ready for the final chapter of the Great Work, *Tikkun*, the repair and mending of the fallen world. Through Tikkun, the Holy Jews will attain the future world, the Utopia, a paradoxical Shangri La of material treasures and blissful existence.

But the Gentile, being a lower caste, even an entirely different species, will remain in the abyss. The Gentile, the goyim (cattle) will serve the superior god-man, the Jew or else he will be killed.

The Serpent as Counselor and Messiah

We read online, in *Beit Ha Derek*, "The Revelation of the Holy Snake," that according to the Kabbalah (*Zohar 11-54a*, Soncino Press Edition), the Serpent is wise and is a counselor to God. Due to the "counsel of the Serpent, four sinless men came into the world:"

> "Four rabbis taught: Four died through the counsel of the Serpent,
> namely, Benjamin, son of Jacob, Amram, the father of Moses,
> Jesse the father of David, and Kilab, the son of David."

In the thirteenth century, Rabbi ben Jacob Ha Cohen wrote that Messiah was, in fact, a snake, or serpent. This belief continued to develop among the religious Jews, especially the rabbis. The study of Gematria, holy math, heightened the doctrine. The Hebrew word for Messiah, *Mashiach*, has the gematria of 358, the same number as *nachash*, the snake. Therefore, it is taught in Judaism that the Messiah *is* the Holy Snake.

Rabbi Yitzchak Ginsburgh, of the Gal Einai Institute (see *inner.org/healing35.htm*), in discussing Amalek, the hated, ancient enemy of the Jews, writes:

> "Just as Amalek represents the epitome of evil, so does the
> positive snake represent the epitome of good. Mashiach (Messiah)
> himself is referred to as the holy snake, as alluded to by the
> phenomenon that the numerical value of Mashiach (358) is the
> same as that of the word for 'snake' (nachash). In the Zohar it is
> told that when the holy snake, Mashiach, will kill the evil snake,
> he will thereby merit to marry the divine princess, to unite with the
> origin of the souls of Israel and so to bring redemption to the
> world."

Ginsburgh's reference to the Holy Snake, or Serpent, killing of the "evil snake" is apparently a reference to Jesus Christ. The killing of

Above: Leviathan, the Holy Serpent as King of the Jews.

Leviathan, protecting the Jewish people (the red circle), from an illuminated 13th century medieval manuscript, around 1280 AD

Jesus, it is taught, will finally result in *Tikkun*, the return of the souls of Israel to their previous heights of glory and their redemption.

The Serpent is the Angel of Help

Rabbi Michael Laitman, of the much recognized Kabbalah Center, speaks of the serpent as the "Angel of Help" ("The Serpent is the Angel of Help," Daily Kabbalah Lesson, Zohar). He says that man encounters the serpent in the lowest region of the Tree of Life, in the abyss where he is introduced to Malkuth, the goddess, divine daughter of the Queen. There, his sexual passions are aroused and "sin crouches at our door," a reference to the Serpent waiting to have sexual relations with Malkuth. This desire by the serpent is a reflection of our own instincts and desires. He writes:

> "The Creator prepared a serpent to help us enter the spiritual world... The serpent comes like an angel sent to us by the Creator... We should be grateful to the serpent for its help.
>
> This snake comes as medication. Indeed, it is not a coincidence that the snake is a symbol of medicine..."

Rabbi Laitman explains that our spiritual growth requires that we rise with the serpent, finding our way toward God *(Ein Sof)* and receiving more and more light.

Jews are People of the Serpent

It is no wonder, given such strange, arcane beliefs, that the Jews are identified as the *"People of the Serpent."*

Rabbi Michael Ezra, in his article, "The Serpent and Its Transformative Power," explains that contrary to the popular understanding that the serpent is evil, the serpent, in fact, has "transformative power in spiritual development."

The serpent, Ezra emphasizes, "symbolically represents our primal drive for ultimate fulfillment" and was originally intended to be "the great servant of man" (*Babylonian Talmud, Sanhedrin 50b*). We must, he states, re-examine the story of the serpent and realize our serpent-like, sexual energy potential. This primal energy, the sex drive, is now suppressed in man, but can be raised and transformed in a positive spiritual path.

> "By channeling our passions toward the spiritual we can transform a potentially destructive drive into one of our most holy and sacred...to achieve the highest Kabbalistic level of human

nature—holiness." (*healing.about.com/od/symbols/a/serpent*)

Rabbi Ezra also emphasizes the *gematria* of the serpent:

"Our sages explain that when two Hebrew words have the same numerical value, they are of the same essence on a more subtle and hidden level... The Hebrew words Mashiach (messiah) and nachash (serpent) have the same numerical value of 358. While on the surface they seem to represent the two diametrically opposed forces of good and evil, they are related in their essence...

"In fact, our tradition explains that when the Messianic era arrives, our primal drive for lust and physical gratification will be removed and everything will be transformed to complete good...the serpent will no longer be coiled and confined (Tikunei-Zohar 21)...

Those of us who allow our primal energy to emerge will enter the doorway to the Divine, travel the road back to the Garden and experience the return to the Temple of God."

We see, then, that the Jewish religion advises the individual to use the Serpent to transform his life, to help him move upward from the abyss into the light. Eventually, it is the serpents help that will enable the Jew to exercise the energy force necessary to emerge into the "doorway to the divine." He will rise from man's fallen state back to the Garden, "and experience the return to the Temple of God."

True Christianity: The Serpent is Adversary and Deceiver

How dramatically different is this devilish philosophy from that of true Christianity, which holds that there is no light, only darkness in the serpent. Indeed, the serpent is not the helper but the dreadful enemy of God and man. Jesus came in the flesh specifically to destroy the works of the serpent, who is Satan, the Adversary and Deceiver.

What is this sick and aberrant religion called "Judaism" that teaches of the supposedly "positive snake," that counsels man to avail himself of the help offered by the serpent, and suggests that man can therewith emerge in the "doorway to the divine" and "return to the Temple of God?"

Jesus willingly died on the cross for our sins and was resurrected into glory. We know this to be true. Therefore, we are free of the works of the devil. As Christians, we do not retain the profane knowledge of the serpent and his evil works in our conscience. He has no place in our lives, and we profoundly reject the counsel of the Jews, namely that the serpent, or Satan, is the "Angel of Help." The scriptures tell us that Jesus "came to set the captives free." And free we are, through His love and sacrifice, His eternal gift to us.

The Jews have rejected this saving grace proffered by Christ Jesus. Consequently, they remain under the tutelage of the serpent. The Jews are, in fact, in *bondage* to Satan and have been "cast out of the kingdom" of God *(Galatians 4)*. Given the fact that the Jews have no persona to help them as they navigate their lives—*Ein Sof*, the supreme being is claimed to have no emotions and is bereft of any direct communicative ability—the Jew seeks out the companionship and guidance of the serpent.

After centuries of reference to the Talmud and the Kabbalah, with almost no counsel sought from the Old Testament, the Jews have embraced the Holy Serpent as their immediate god of help and as "medication." He is the one who guides their paths toward the Light. Through his aid and assistance, the Jew progressively learns how to cope with the outside world. He has become dependent on the Holy Serpent, Satan.

The Holy Serpent is indeed the "God" of the Jews. As Harold Rosenthal, politician and top assistant to New York Senator Jacob Javits, said in a provocative interview, "Most Jews do not like to admit it, but our God is Lucifer... We are his chosen people. Lucifer is very much alive" (*The Hidden Tyranny*, 1976).

Lucifer is the Serpent

Lucifer is another name for the infernal Satan. Helena Blavatsky, the Russian Jew and founder of Theosophy, a religious system affiliated with and patterned on the Kabbalah, states:

> "Thus the true and uncompromising Kabbalists admit that, for all
> the purposes of science and philosophy, it is enough that the
> profane should know that the great magic agent...is that which the
> Church calls *Lucifer*, the vehicle of light and the receptacle of all

the forms, a force spread throughout the whole universe, with its direct and indirect works, into Satan and his works…"

Blavatsky further reveals that Lucifer is the *Astral Light* and the *Mysterious Magnum* (Great Mystery). The modern-day Jewish religion agrees, holding up Satan as he who guides the Jews forward into more light and toward the Divine. He is, we shall discover, the protection and covering for the Jewish nation across the globe. As the Holy Serpent, his eye (*Ayin*) is ever awake, watching and all-seeing. So complete, so enmeshed is the figure of Satan, the Holy Serpent, in their religion, that the Jewish Kabbalist reports him to be the *covering serpent* and the Jew is himself identified as the *"Serpent within the serpent."*

Congregation of the Dead

It is, as Jesus said, as recorded in *Matthew 32*, "God is not the God of the dead, but of the living." The Jews, because of their unbelief and their stubbornness and stiff necks, were not of the living, but were numbered among the dead. They were, as the prophet Isaiah commented, the "Congregation of the dead" and so they worshipped then—and worship today—the ruler of the dead, known to be Satan, the Holy Serpent.
Jesus said of the Jews:

"Woe unto you, scribes and Pharisees, hypocrites! for ye are like unto whited sepulchres, which indeed appear beautiful outward, but are within full of dead men's bones, and of all uncleanness…

Wherefore ye be witnesses unto yourselves, that ye are the children of them which killed the prophets.

Fill ye up then the measure of your fathers.

Ye serpents, ye generation of vipers, how can ye escape the damnation of hell?"

Significantly, Christian martyr Stephen, in *Acts 7:43* had the pulse of God when he reminded the Jews that they had not changed over the course of the centuries, but continued in their rebellion against God to that very day. Stephen declared:

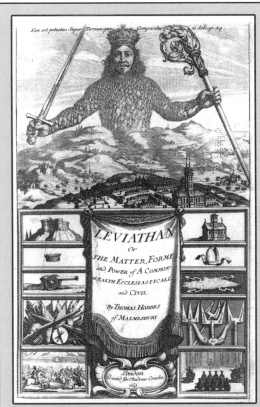

Frontispiece for the book *Leviathan*, by Thomas Hobbes, depicting the coming King of the Jews, the beast from the sea, rising and holding a sword and a rod, the symbol of royal power in his hands.

Below: The horrible image of Leviathan the serpent from a 1989 movie.

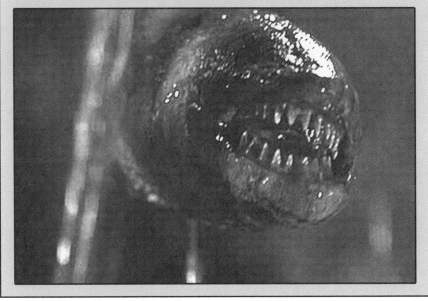

"Yea, ye took up the tabernacle of Moloch and the Star of your god; Remphan, figures which ye made to worship them, and I will carry you away beyond Babylon."

"Beyond Babylon!" that is where their hatred and rejection of the loving Jesus Christ, Messiah of the whole world, is taking the Jews. "Beyond Babylon"—that is the ultimate destination of the ones who claim to be holier than God and chosen by Him; that is the destiny of the unrepentant Israel, the "People of the Serpent."

FOUR

Triumph of the Holy Serpent: Nothing Sacred—The Truth About Judaism

"Jews are not expected to believe in anything in particular…"
— Rabbi Martin Siegel

"The fundamental characteristic feature of the Jewish religion…is solely materialistic."
— Werner Sombert
German Philosopher

C onsider: Judaism has no real and ultimate "God" whom the Jews can talk to, hear from, know, or even approach. In Judaism, there is officially no "Supreme Being."

Can Judaism, then, truly be a "religion" if there is no Supreme Being who can be reached, no Deity who personally cares for the individual?

The most holy book of the Jews is *The Babylonian Talmud* and, admittedly, it is written by *men*, pharisees appointed by earthly agencies as "Rabbis."

Even the Torah and the Old Testament is interpreted and understood only through the lenses of the rabbis. Every word, every letter, must be put under the microscope to be evaluated by the rabbis according to kabbalistic formulae. And who is author of the Kabbalah? Why, that would once again be... the rabbis.

Jesus said, moreover, that the Jews actually *nullify* the commandments of God with their man-made *traditions*, the same pharisaic traditions found today in the Talmud and Kabbalah.

Jews have no real "personal God." God is definitely an abstraction in the Jewish religion. Unable to pray to him, they petition instead the Goddess (known as *Shekinah*, the Divine Presence), whom they suppose is constantly having sex with God and with the Holy Serpent. Perhaps she will listen to their pleas for aid. Or there are the other Sephirot (gods) of the Kabbalah, like Hesod (the phallis and sun) or Malkuth, yet another goddess, the tenth sephirot at the lower end of the abyss.

Many Jews Pray to Satan

Many Jews literally pray to Satan, or they simply refer to their theocracy, the rabbi, or rabbis, who rule over them. These are the Elders, and they have power and authority over every aspect of the pious Jew's life. The rabbis, of course, depend on the Talmud to make all their decisions. In Islam, the Moslems rely on Sharia Law; in Judaism, the governing entity, or rulebook, is the Talmud, its 613 laws and its commentaries.

Mullins, in *Mullins' New History of the Jews*, writes, "The fact is that the Jews have never been much concerned with God. In the Old Testament, God speaks most frequently to reproach the Jews for their crimes against humanity."

The fact that Judaism is a religion of man-made traditions has caused many to claim that Judaism is all a "con." It is said to be a fake religion designed by Jews *for* Jews. The theology of Judaism is the quest for material and economic gain. The ultimate goal of world conquest and the setting up of world government—led by and for Jews, of course— certainly leads one to this conclusion.

Rabbi Martin Siegel notes: "Jews are not expected to believe in anything in particular precisely because the emphasis (in Judaism) is on a universal community."

Now it is interesting to note that the Judaic religion comprises a hodgepodge of petty, bewildering rules: Drink this; don't drink that; eat this; don't eat that, etc. There are even rules on how to use the toilet properly. In all there are 613 laws in the Talmud and these and other rules comprise the Halakhah. But every Jewish sect—the Lubavitchers, the Sephardim, etc., has its own unique set of regulations it has added to the witches brew.

Nevertheless, on things that *really* matter—for example, man's relationship to God, who God is, where He is and about heaven and hell, there are few defining clauses. No strict set of rules. The Jew is left alone, without a navigation tool, so to speak.

A Community of Jews for Jews

In other words, whatever will lend itself to achieving the goal of a universal community and to enjoying one's life is consistent with the Judaic religion. That is why so many Jews in America and Europe claim to support *"whatever is good for Israel."*

This means that the indigenous, local culture is debased by the Jew, nationalism is de-emphasized, other religions are scoffed at, immigration is encouraged, trade and business is internationalized, and foreign policy is promoted over strictly local development. That is why the United States, due to the influence of powerful Jewish lobbies, has engaged in war after war overseas, has entered into numerous self-effacing trade agreements, has sponsored massive immigration shifts, and has corrupted the Christian religion and American traditional culture. These effects are positive for the Jews and aligned with the Judaic global plan for domination.

The neocon determination to control U.S. politics is waged strictly on behalf of whatever is good for Israel. However, this aggressive pro-Israel policy by neocons is often adamantly denied, lest the people of America discover they are being "played" by the Jews.

Jewish Religion is Solely Materialistic

The emphasis, then, by Judaism is, again, *"whatever is good for Israel."* This emphasis expresses itself not in man's life and spiritual state *after death* but on the here and now. Jews do not lust for heavenly rewards but for economic progress and earthly treasure now. Thus, famous Jewish philosopher Werner Sombert, in *The Economic Life of Jews*, p. 227, writes:

> "The fundamental characteristic feature of the Jewish religion
> consists in the fact that is a religion which has nothing to do with
> the other world, but, as one might say, is solely materialistic..."

The communist Karl Marx emphasized that, "The god of the Jews is money." In a short book he wrote on the topic of Jews and money, Marx wrote:

> "The (Jewish) god of practical needs and private interests is money. Money degrades all the (other) gods of mankind and turns them into commodities."

Marx believed that the Jews were emancipated precisely because they looked to no nation or religion to guide them. Israel's religion and nation were, in a word, "money!"

Heinrich Heine, German philosopher and a Jew, shortened the discussion by concluding, "The god of the Jew is money, and Rothschild is his prophet." We see, then, that "whatever" is good for Israel is also whatever is good for the bankers, and the global banking system is based on usury and is operated by Jews, for Jews.

Money is the End Goal of the Jew

The divine presence in the world, according to the Jews, is therefore a mysticism of *Shekinah* wisdom or glory. Shekinah is another name for the feminine deity of Malkuth in the Jewish Tree of Life, one of the ten sephifirot (gods) of the Kabbalah. This Shekinah glory is believed to permeate the world, infusing it with Jewish energy and creativeness. Sexuality and other human characteristics are subsumed under this Shekinah wisdom, but chief is money. Money is the end goal of the Jew. The love of money is his primary preoccupation.

No wonder the Apostle Paul, in his letter to Timothy in the New Testament, stated, *"The love of money is the root of all evil."*

The Holy Serpent Makes the Jews Gods

It is important for us to note that *Malkuth*, the goddess figure in the kabbalist Tree of Life, is the same as the feminine spirit known as *Shekinah*. And the Shekinah cannot be separated from the spirit of the great serpent. Thus, the Holy Serpent of the Jews is, in fact, one and the same as the Shekinah glory.

The *Holy Serpent* (also called *Leviathan*) moves man with sexual lust and ravages his mind with the inordinate desire for money. Judaism is a phallic/vaginal cult of sex fueled by a lust for moneymaking. This insane thrust of Judaism is its inspiration for the Holy Serpent, the Jewish Messiah, to rise up out of the abyss (the pit), taking the Jew worshiper to newer and newer heights of moral corruption and degradation until he, or she, attains the Tree of Life position of Kether (the Crown).

At that point the Holy Serpent, as Messiah, having given the Jews their long-sought World Kingdom, is devoured by the Jews in a spectacular orgy and feast in which savage bloodletting and the eating of human flesh is front and center. This is Utopia for the Jews, a light-filled paradise existence, signaled by a Holy Communion of sorts, and a celebration of self-divinity. Finally, the Jews will have their Kingdom. They will be its gods and they will be represented by a man King, like David, who rises from their midst.

Every Jew, however, will also act as his own king and every Gentile will serve him as slave. Rabbi Emmanuel Rabinovich, in 1952, addressing a group of European rabbis, exclaimed:

> "The god for which you have striven so concertedly for 3,000 years is at last within our reach… Our race will take its rightful place in the world, with every Jew a king, and every Gentile a slave."

Rabinovich reminded the rabbis that, when the Kingdom has come, whites (non-Jews) will be forbidden to marry whites, bringing about a multiracial world, a mongrel-like polyglot of races. The universal Kingdom will have displaced the nations, making patriotism and nationalism obsolete.

"Our most dangerous enemy (the white man) will become only a memory."

Plainly, Jews do not view themselves as "white" and they reject their placement in this genetic pile. They are, they suppose, a unique and special species, i.e. god-men.

The Present and Future Trajectory of Judaism

This, then, is the ultimate goal of World Jewry—global domination, meaning sex, money, and power on an unparalleled scale. But what is Judaism today as it survives for this supposedly lofty aspirational goal? A fascinating book written recently (2003) by Douglas Rushkoff entitled *Nothing Sacred—The Truth About Judaism* examines not only Judaism as it is practiced today but also surveys the future for Judaism and the Jew. Rushkoff, an ardent Jew, is a commentator for National Public Radio (NPR). He writes for the Public Broadcasting System (PBS), authors essays for *Time*, and has won numerous literary awards.

Here is Rushkoff's summation of what the religion of Judaism and its traditions are today:

"…they (the Judaic gods) are not parents. We…are the parents here."

"Judaism contains the seeds of an extraordinarily progressive process that strikes out at blind faith"

"…obsession with intermarriage"

"(Judaism) invites inquiry and change. It is a tradition born out of revolution, committed to evolution, and always willing to undergo renaissance at a moments notice"

"Judaism can be…reinterpreted…for a new era… It is…a continuation of the Jewish tradition for collaborative reinvention"

"Jewish institutions are reorganizing themselves to function more like the…massive global corporations and (uses) their commercial expressions on the human people"

"The Talmud (allows Jews) to reinterpret a biblical myth in order to support an idea."

"The Jews unique position as perpetual outsiders led them to adopt and promote a wide range of cosmopolitan and inclusive business standards and ethical practices."

"Their (the Jews') specialties became banking and

communications... money, interest and brokerage."

"As Jewish political theorists such as Karl Marx understood, the education of the masses is a prerequisite..."

"A fluid society with ever-changing boundaries served (the Jews) better than a closed or static one in which outsiders and new ideas are feared..."

"Anti-Semites are not entirely unfounded in their claim that Jews are behind a great media conspiracy... Jews interest in the film, television, and entertainment industries found its roots in... early survival imperatives and cultural goals."

"Jews dedication to expanding the role of media in peoples' lives... is (intended) to promote... the value of pluralism... Like all good communication, media tends to call sacred values into question."

"Media is a form of mass education."

"...the more inclusive and tolerant a society, the more likely it was to include the Jews..."

"The most central prayer, the sh'ma ("The Lord is One"), amounts to a declaration of the unity of the universe...."

"...under a single, abstract God. By keeping God unnamable and unknowable, Jews could also keep this deity universal."

"Halakhah (Jewish law or code of behavior) brings divinity into one's daily activities... As a result, Judaism became less of something a person believed in than something one did."

"God must, ultimately, be a universal and nameless God...an abstract and unknowable deity."

"The natural result of settling for an abstract and unknowable deity is then to focus, instead on human beings and life itself as the supremely sacred vessels of existence."

"There's no one around to pray to, so one learns to enact sanctity through ethical behavior."

"Most Jewish thinkers have understood God more by what he is not than by whatever he is."

"Medieval philosopher (and famous rabbi) Moses Maimonides developed what is now called 'negative theology.' God is not a creature. God has no hands, and neither does God have emotions."

"For all practical purposes, he (God) does not exist...God is just not something Jews are supposed to worry about... Jews focus on an external master whose edicts they need to obey is replaced by an emphasis on peoples' duty to one another."

"God doesn't need worship. Jews evolve their concept of him, and their relationship to him, merely as a means toward implementing more human ways of living."

"The God of the prophets shuns direct worship in favor of a more internally felt divinity...More primitive and concretized experiences of God almost always lead to human suffering."

"The Jewish God's recession from human affairs—and human belief systems—has been all but preordained by the Jewish religion."

Atheism the Prevailing Belief in Judaism

What we see in Rushkoff's elemental explanation of the Jewish religion is that, bluntly spoken, Judaism is an expression of *atheism*. Yes, Jews are atheists. Their god is unknowable, unnamed; He has "recessed" from human affairs. He doesn't need worship; in fact, He "shuns" it. He has "no emotions."

As Rushkoff states, *"For all practical purposes, God does not exist... God is just not something Jews are supposed to worry about."*

What a monumental display of hubris by Jews! Rejecting a loving, personal God, the Jews say that "God" is an abstraction, something they *do* rather than serve and worship. Their fealty and loyalty is to each other as human beings—they believe the right word for Jews is human "gods"—and refer to their own "internally felt divinity."

This is the New Age Lie: evolved humans are as gods, exercising right and wrong as only they see fit. It is the Crowleyian motto once again, *"Do What Thou Wilt Shall be the Whole of the Law."*

The only requirement for the individual Jew is that he or she must serve "Social Justice." He must perform and "do" a mitzvah, a good work. But good works are reserved primarily for other Jews. The Gentile deserves no good works. The Gentile, the Goyim, are like cattle, and their existence, says Rabbi Ovadia Yosef, the late Chief Rabbi of Israel, is meant only to serve the Jews, their masters.

This, then, is a recipe for great evil. A narcissistic religion without a god, self-based, without faith and with works only for the limited members of one's blood kind.

It is, moreover, a religion in which its adherents do not look to the hereafter. There are no heavenly rewards. Thus the greedy attitude of take everything you can in this life is fostered. The focus of Judaism, Rushkoff reveals, is "on human beings and life itself as the supremely sacred."

No God to Hear Prayers

Nor is there a God in heaven who hears ones prayers and petitions. *"There's no one around to pray to,"* says Rushkoff. This creates a feeling of hopelessness, as the Jew realizes he is all alone in the here and now. Since there is no real God in heaven to pray to and turn to in time of need, the Jew has invented the many lesser deities of Kabbalah, even the Holy Serpent. Worse, Lucifer is often the object of prayer and Jews pray alternately both to a kabbalistic god (or goddess) or to Lucifer, considered a "helping angel" in Judaism.

To put it in stark terms, since there is no God to turn to, Jews pray to whatever entity that will provide solace and real help in time of need. This is a prime example of dialectical thinking, of Maimonides' idea of "negative theology."

In the Soviet Union, we saw what happened when a predominately Jewish cult, the communist party, proclaiming themselves "atheists," purged and slaughtered some 66 million innocent, mostly Christian citizens. Jews came from all over the globe to help build this supposed, new "Jewish Utopia." Synagogues and rabbis were everywhere favored— some 70% of the thousands of Soviet gulag prison camps were run by commandants who were also rabbis! Seventeen of the first nineteen members of the Soviet Politburo were Jews. Communist leader Vladimir Lenin and his deputy, Leon Trotsky, were both Jews. Yagoda, the first leader of the secret police, was a Jew.

These monsters said they were doing good works. They sought to "heal the earth," to spread communism through Tikkun Olam, and equality—brotherhood of man—throughout the planet, beginning with the Soviet Union and its republics. All aims of Judaic spirits.

As Douglas Rushkoff informs us in his pivotal book, *Nothing Sacred—The Truth About Judaism*, the Jews collectively have a "responsibility" to heal the earth. Is that what motivated Karl Marx, whose ideas spawned communism, and Vladimir Lenin, the Father of communism in Soviet Russia? Each shared a "responsibility" to heal the earth, to bring about Tikkun Olam, the mending or repair of the earth through "creative destruction." Here's how Rushkoff, in his book, describes this concept of a future Jewish Utopia based on "Social Justice:"

> "The concept of *Tikkun Olam* or healing the earth…is a poetic way of expressing the responsibility Jews have to 'heal the earth.' (It is) a mandate for social justice on behalf of the whole planet."

Was Tikkun Olam, with all its blood, sweat, and tears, as achieved in real life in the communist world from 1917 to, say 1986, a superb triumph of the Holy Serpent of Judaism? Are there more victories of the Holy Serpent to come?

FIVE

The Holy Serpent a Chameleon

The Rabbinical Religion of Man-Made Traditions

"For laying aside the commandment of God, ye hold the tradition of men..."

— Jesus Christ
Mark 7:8

"Making the word of God of none effect through your tradition..."

— Jesus Christ
Mark 7:13

"Beware lest any man spoil you through philosophy and vain deceit, after the tradition of men, after the rudiments of the world, and not after Christ."

— Paul,
Colossians 2:8

The chameleon is a creature, a lizard, that can change its color and appearance as nature or need dictate. He can be brown, tan, green, or even red, or colors in between. The Holy Serpent, too, can deceptively change. He also persuades others also to change their doctrine. As the environment changes, so do the lies of his followers. What is good and righteous in one era or condition becomes evil and polluted in another. What is sin to one rabbi is justified as necessary, even a virtue to another. There are few absolutes in Judaism.

Such is not the case in Christianity. Most Christians hold to the belief that they must follow rules and strictures of the Holy Bible. What Jesus said is true; those things He condemned are wrong. In today's confused and lukewarm world, the Christian religion also is confused. Yet, the commandments of Christ and the Apostles are firm and never changing.

Judaism A Man-Made Religion

Consider, however, the Judaic System. Many Christians think the laws and rules of Judaism are found set in concrete in the Old Testament. This is not Judaism. Even the words of the Old Testament are subject to interpretation, according to the traditions of rabbis. Judaism is a system of rabbinical laws, and some 613 are set forth in the Talmud. And who authored the Talmud? Why, rabbis, of course, it is formed by the *traditions* of men.

So, too, the Kabbalah and its books are written by Jews. Both the Kabbalah and the Talmud were developed and amplified in Babylon, during the captivity of the Jews. The Talmud is even formally titled, *The Babylonian Talmud*. These were, at first, oral in nature. Later, they were written down and transcribed, but at no time has the claim been made that the teachings of Talmud and Kabbalah are direct from the hand or mouth of "God."

The Jews High God Cannot be Known or Approached

Indeed, as we have seen, there is no *known* deity to which the Jews can ascribe anything. *Ein Sof*, their high God, does not communicate directly with men. He has many emanations—we can call them gods and goddesses—arrayed in the Tree of Life of the Kabbalah. While Jews do often pray to one or another of these deities, their Talmud and Kabbalah are authored by the rabbis.

Ein Sof, the high "God" of the Kabbalah, cannot communicate directly to followers. He does not love or hate. He is a neutral energy Force. Henry Wilson Coil, a high-level Mason and author of the authoritative, *Coil's Masonic Encyclopedia*, points out how Jews and their Masonic cohorts depict this so-called "God:"

"Men have to decide whether they want a God like the ancient
Hebrew Yahweh, a partisan tribal God, with whom they can talk...
or a boundless, eternal, universal, undenominational, and
international Divine Spirit so vastly removed from the speck called
Man that he cannot be known, named, or approached."

Coil makes plain that he and other Masons (and Jews!) prefer the
unapproachable, non-personal, unknowable God. Note that Coil says this
"God" is not named and cares not for the welfare of individual men, who
are described by Coil as "specks." That is why, in the Jewish religion,
"God" has no name and He is spelled G-d, the letter o being omitted. In
effect the Jewish chief deity is not a real, caring God. Therefore, the
Serpent takes his place as helper Messiah and the Jew eventually becomes
his own Messiah and, collectively, his own God.

Judaism thus is a rabbinical religion. It is based on the *traditions* of
men. It is a man-made religion, unlike any other. Indeed, Jesus told the
Jewish religious leaders that they had rejected and became separated
from the commandments of God, and instead, held the *tradition* of men
(Mark 7:8). Christ emphasized that the Jews even *nullified* the word of
God, "making the word of God of none effect through your *tradition*"
(Mark 7:13).

The Apostle Paul Warns of the Jewish Traditions

The Apostle Paul, well aware of the machinations of the Jews through
their traditions, cautioned Christians to avoid these make-believe fables
of the rabbinical sect:

> *"Beware lest any man spoil you through philosophy and vain deceit,*
> *after the tradition of men, after the rudiments of the world, and not*
> *after Christ" (Colossians 2:8).*

Now, read again what Paul said. He wryly observed that a person can
be taken captive by philosophy and empty deceit. Don't be taken *captive*,
don't lose the ability to cast sound judgement, by listening to and
believing the false teachings of tradition being pushed by the rabbis, he
advised.

But Paul also tells the Christian that the traditions of men given by
the rabbis were more than mere formulations of unwise or corrupt rabbis.

No, these traditions—the ones recommended and even ruled mandatory for the Jews—are "according to the elemental spirits of the world..." They are conceived and are the evil ideas put forth by demon spirits.

Christians often write and ask me, "Texe, can I not study and use the best parts of the Kabbalah?" Some also want to read and follow the Talmud, imagining the 613 laws must have some good to be followed. How foolish are these Christians! Please take the words of Paul seriously. The Talmud and the Kabbalah are the writing of devils. They are intended to mangle your mind. There is no good in them. They will turn out to be twisted and perverted. *These are the inventions of demon spirits.*

In reading and studying the Talmud and Kabbalah, you are disobeying Jesus' words. Can anything good come out of disobedience?

Some men and women are led by God to study these pharisaic laws and magical superstitions in order to expose them. Fine, but by no means imagine you will become a more wise or better Christian through these horrific prescriptions.

The Talmud a Tool of Manipulation and Jewish Supremacy

It is interesting that the Talmud is a system of Jewish rabbinic commentaries. Sometimes in the Talmud we discover that rabbis disagree. Again, as I explained, Judaism is a dynamic (ever-changing) religion. In fact, Judaism is made up of several competing belief systems. These are similar to Christian denominations. One can be a member of the Orthodox sect, or be a conservative Jew, or a Reform Jew. And within each of these groups, there are sub-sects and different beliefs.

It is, however, the Orthodox who run the nation of Israel. They pass the legislative laws and generally dictate the culture. Their control is not binding on all, however, and debate is vigorous in political and other matters. The secular Jew also is a large segment of the Jewish public. But whatever is one's religious "flavor," almost all Jews adhere to the basic tenets of the Talmud, and many are now into the Kabbalah. In fact, many elements of the Kabbalah are submerged *into* the Talmud.

Thus, almost every Jew sanctions the basic Talmudic evils. Most are convinced that Jews are a special species, superior to all other races, God's Chosen People, heirs of the whole world. Thus, we can say without being dogmatic, that as a whole, Jews believe in the coming Jewish Utopia, a time when the Jew will be given all the world's wealth, the Jews will, during the Utopia (known as the *Messianic*, or *Kingdom Age*),

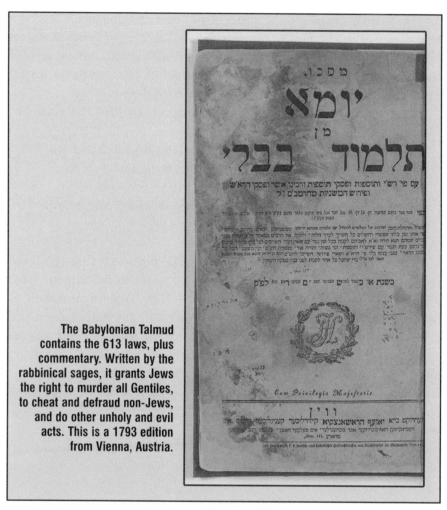

The Babylonian Talmud contains the 613 laws, plus commentary. Written by the rabbinical sages, it grants Jews the right to murder all Gentiles, to cheat and defraud non-Jews, and do other unholy and evil acts. This is a 1793 edition from Vienna, Austria.

be the masters and the Gentiles will be their slaves.

A Dangerous Collective of Deranged Individuals

As you can see, this is an extremely xenophobic and narcissistic people. Given this almost universal attribute, the Jews are a dangerous collective of deranged individuals. As the Jews progress in their insane goal to destroy other cultures and work to extend their own control over peoples and governments, the danger will greatly increase. We have seen what the effects of Jews and their sick rabbinical religion have been on millions of Russians and others during the communist era. We have also seen the horrors inflicted on the pitiful poor of downtrodden Palestine. Massacres, torture, manifest evil are the product of Jews and Judaism. This is a historical fact and cannot be disregarded. It is the Judaic religion and its tradition that justifies—in the minds of the Jewish people—these terrible atrocities. The Jew, in murdering and mistreating the Gentile, is simply fulfilling his and the inferior Gentiles appointed destiny.

De Poncins, in *The Vatican and Freemasonry* (p. 76-77), writes:

> "The oneness of the human race, the goal toward which Judaism
> and Freemasonry work hand in hand...is the unification of the
> world under Jewish law... The nations will be converted to
> Judaism and will obey the law or else they will be destroyed, and
> the Jews will be masters of the world."

The New Age movement's fancy and high-sounding goals of universal oneness and Freemasonry's brotherhood and equality are mere elements of propaganda. Virtually every New Age organization is founded and led by religious Jews. The Jews tell only half-truths. Once fully within the system, the initiate discovers that godhead, higher consciousness, and of course, unity and diversity, etc. are all subject to his acceptance of the requirements of Judaic tradition. The New Age Gentile must be "converted" to Judaism according to the Noahide Laws spelled out in the Talmud...or else he will be killed.

SIX

The Serpent Force and the Jewish Covenant With Death

"Dan shall be a serpent by the way, an adder in the path, that biteth the horse heels, so that his rider shall fall backward."

— Genesis 49:17

The Jewish Kabbalah, a major component of the religion of Judaism, has universal appeal. When the Jews of Israel were taken captive centuries ago by Babylon's Nebuchadnezzar, the rabbis studied the Mystery religions of the Babylonians. The strange concepts they discovered were not unique to Babylon, but had come from the Egyptians and others. Indeed, these mystical teachings—and worship of serpents—had spread throughout Asia and even to the Americas, where the Incas, the Aztecs, and others worshipped in the same manner. The Greeks and Romans, too, adopted the same gods and goddesses, adored various forms of the serpent and practiced the Babylonian religion.

So the rabbis borrowed these Mystery religion practices and brought them back with them to a restored Israel in the days of Nehemiah. When Jesus came, he found that the *Traditions of the Elders* involved many of these beliefs, for example, reincarnation and transmigration of souls.

It was only in the 13th century, however, that the Jews began to write down the ancient religious principles they had much earlier adopted and spread orally. Rabbi Moses de Leon, a Spanish Jew, is given credit for the *Zohar*, one of the chief books where the secret knowledge of the Kabbalah is found. The Renaissance period in the 15th century was a fertile time when Popes and Gentile intellectuals began to be fascinated with the books of the Kabbalah. Today, of course, the Kabbalah is prominent in Judaism, accepted enthusiastically by most rabbis and even quoted extensively by apostate "Christian" rabbis and pastors.

Freemasonry is a Branch of Judaism

The Kabbalah is the basis for the Church of Satan's doctrinal teachings and is fount for the heresies of the New Age cults and religions. But it is in Freemasonry, a worldwide network of Lodges and secret societies, where the Kabbalah has really engineered an amazing transformation. While the Masonic Lodge has its own unique programs of propaganda and indoctrination, in essence, the Masonic Lodge is a branch of Judaism.

Let me repeat that. The Masonic Lodge is nothing less than a branch of Judaism. The men who join the Lodge are not told this in lower degrees, but, in fact, they are made familiar with the religion of the Jews as they enter upon their career as a Mason. They will discover that the Masonic Compass is but a stylized six-pointed star. They will see that all the symbols of the Lodge come out of Judaism and that even the names of the 33 ritual ceremonies are Judaic.

The mention of the name of Jesus is pointedly prohibited in Masonic rituals, understandable since, in Judaism, the name of Jesus is anathema.

The Encyclopedia of Freemasonry explains the Judaic nature of the Masonic Lodge. On page 769, in the entry for the Temple of Solomon, is revealed this fact:

> "Each lodge is and must be a symbol of the Jewish Temple; each
> Master (Mason) in the chain is a representative of the Jewish king;
> and every Mason is a personation of the Jewish workman."

A well-versed Christian scholar, studying the Masonic Lodge and its relationship to the religion of Judaism, wrote to me his astute conclusion on this matter:

> "Texe, do you realize what this means? Let's examine: Each
> Lodge a symbol of the Jewish Temple. Each Lodge contains the

spirit of antichrist and all the occult Kabbalah forces in the Temple.

"Now, each Lodge, globally, has been pre-positioned for world government emergence of Solomon's Temple. As a result, the very real State Religion of Masonry is in place, around the world, now preparing for World Government. (Examples: Masons made school administrators, governors, Senators, and Congressmen, on state and federal levels...)"

Most Gentile members of the Masonic Lodge remain ignorant of their deep involvement in Judaism. They have been brainwashed to believe that all things Jewish are acceptable, since, they are convinced, Judaism is simply a reflection of the Old Testament. They are unaware that they are being introduced to a Mystery religion and are steadily progressing in the Kabbalistic knowledge.

In their acceptance of Judeo-Freemasonry, the Masons have become full members of the *Synagogue of Satan*. After all, this satanic institution is made up of "them which say they are Jews and are not, but *are* the Synagogue of Satan" (see *Revelation 2* and *3*).

No wonder, then, that kabbalistic rabbis count the millions of members of the Masonic Lodges as simply Gentile dupes, easily led, eventually to be swallowed up in the gaping, open mouth of the Holy Serpent!

The Masonic Lodge Rituals Based on the Kabbalah

Albert Pike, former Sovereign Grand Commander of Scottish Rite Freemasonry, is only one of the many Masonic authorities to report that the Masonic Lodge and its rituals are based on the Jewish Kabbalah. "Freemasonry," concludes Masonic expert Paul Foster Case (*The Masonic Letter G*, Macoy Publishing and Masonic Supply Company, Richmond, VA, 1981), "has been developed in its present form by persons having some acquaintance with the Hebrew system of occult philosophy known as the qabalah (or Kabbalah)."

The three pillars which support the Lodge and the Masonic ideas related to Hiram Abiff—a christ-like figure in Masonry—are said to have been derived from the Kabbalah. They are taken directly from the kabbalistic diagram of the *Tree of Life* which also contains ten aspects (or deities) of divine emanation. These ten aspects are called *Sephiroth*.

"The whole Tree, with its ten numbers and 22 (Hebrew) letters represents the thirty-two paths of wisdom. Kabbalists regard it of such importance that they declare it to be the key to all things." (Paul Foster Case, *The Masonic Letter G*, pp. 15-16)

Dan and the Serpent

Freemasonry further notes that the Mason's "sacred name," *Abaddon*, means Father of Dan in Hebrew. It also stands for *"Destroyer."* Moreover, *Ab* itself means the number 3. Thus Abaddon, the King of demons who escapes out of the fiery bottomless pit (*Revelation 9*) is a *triple monarch*. This signifies that he represents Father, Son, and Mother, the unholy trinity of the occult world. Therefore Abaddon is the totality of evil: *Abaddon is Satan, the Serpent.*

Dan, of course, was leader of one of the original tribes of Israel. In a telling prophecy given by his father, Jacob on his deathbed, it was prophesied that Dan would judge his people. It was further prophesied:

"Dan shall be a serpent by the way, an adder in the path, that biteth the horse heels, so that his rider shall fall backward." (Genesis 49:17)

There is much more I could say about Dan, including the fact that he and his tribe are not one of the 12 tribes of 12,000 each (144,000) to be saved in the last days, as listed in the book of *Revelation*.

Also, in the scriptures we find that Dan was first assigned the *Serpent* as his tribe's ensign. Rejecting this ensign, Dan defiantly chose the *eagle* to be his ensign.

Dan went on to be a conqueror and to expand his tribe's land and territory through military force. Dan was certainly a greedy and evil man, and he deserved the Serpent as his ensign.

Dan, then, is a Serpent and Abbadon is the Father of this Serpent. This is the Holy Serpent of Judaism and the Kabbalah. It is theorized that the latter days antichrist will come from the tribe of Dan and that, as the antichrist, he will, indeed, bring judgment upon his people, Israel.

The Meaning of the Masonic "G"

In his revealing book, *The Masonic Letter G*, Mason Paul Foster Case meticulously explains the Kabbalistic meaning of the letter G in

Freemasonry. The lower adepts are first told it stands for "God" or for the "Grand Architect." Later, they are informed it also means "Geometry." But higher initiates discover its true meaning:

> "G, however, is the initial of God. Its Greek equivalent is the
> initial of *Gaia*, the earth mother, eldest born of Chaos, whose
> name is the root of the noun *geometria*, geometry…Gimel, the
> Hebrew correspondence to G… *gadol*, majesty and *gebur*, strong."

But, says Case, there is more. G is the initial of a Rabbinical term "regarded by the wise men of Israel as being the alphabetical sign of the triangular *delta* and it is connected with the Hebrew letter *yod*," which means esoterically, the *phallus of God*. This gives an indication of its clearly *sexual* nature.

Case goes on to explain that, for the Hebrews, the *sanctum sanctorum* of the Temple was the actual dwelling place of the Divine presence or Shekinah. The Shekinah is the bride, or feminine consort of Ein Sof, the Jews' ineffable, highest God.

The geometrical shape of both the perfect Masonic Lodge and the Temple is that of a *cube*. According to the *Sefer Yetzirah*, a book of the Kabbalah, "the place of God is the interior center (the *sanctum sanctorum*) from which radiate the *six* boundless lines establishing space, and sealed with the six permutations of the divine name, *Yeho*. A cube is a solid, bounded by six equal faces."

Though Case doesn't make this point, it can easily be seen that combined, we have a grand total of six, six, and six, or 666.

The Bible says that the temple was erected to honor the mysterious name of Deity. Kabbalistic rabbis may infer that in regards to gematria, the number of his name is *666*. This correlates exactly with *Revelation 13:18*:

> *"Here is wisdom. Let him that hath understanding count the number*
> *of the beast: for it is the number of a man; and his number is Six*
> *hundred threescore and six."*

Are there other mysteries we can infer from study of the esoteric letter G? Indeed, there are. I have said that the G stands for the *Delta* triangle and therefore is a symbol of Deity. The Delta is the *feminine*

The Masonic square and compass is a stylized Jewish six-pointed star. The G inside stands for the "phallus of Deity." The symbol as a whole stands for the sex act between man and woman. Freemasonry, like its parent sect, Judaism, is a phallic cult.

triangle, the lower half of the Masonic Compass and it is mounted on top by the masculine triangle to complete the Masonic sign of the double triangle.

However, the G is also connected to the letter *Yod*. Case writes:

"It is well understood by Kabbalists that though the name of the letter *yod* means hand, the letter is really an emblem of that divine power of creation in its own image belonging to Deity. Thus, yod represents what the Greek's called the *phallus*, the male organ of *generation...*"

Thus, the letter G ultimately stands for the sex act between the highest Hebrew Deity, *Ein Sof*, and his Shekinah, the Divine Presence. Case says that the G—meaning *phallus* of Deity—"may seem to be indelicate," but that Masons are proud of this link to the ancient Mysteries.

Mackey, publisher of the *Encyclopedia of Freemasonry*, writes:

"The phallus, therefore, as the symbol of the male generative principle, was very universally venerated among the ancients, and that, too, as a religious rite, without the slightest reference to any

Mysteries and is common today in the tantric yoga of the Hindus. It is, says Case:

> "The processes whereby a man may so perfect and ripen his own consciousness, may so purify and change his own body, that he may have the same direct awareness of his immortal part (the phallus) that was attained by our ancient brethren, are the real secrets of Freemasonry. They are indicated with sufficient detail and clearness in the rites and symbols of the Craft Lodge degrees.

So we have it direct from the Masonic authorities themselves, who exalt and hold sacred the practices of the Kabbalah, a foundation of modern Judaism. Sex is the pathway to godhood for the man who would become a god. This "indelicate" process is the *Serpent Force*; it is the ultimate Chokmah, or wisdom of the Jew.

This so-called "secret" to attaining Jewish power shows us just how far the practitioner of today's Judaism has come from the godly principles of the Abrahamic and Mosaic Covenants. The Serpent Force is now being touted as the process by which the individual is made a "member of the covenant."

Abaddon Rising

Revelation 9 tells us that Abaddon, the King of devils, will one day soon come up out of the fiery, bottomless pit, which is hell. He will rise up amidst smoke in Jerusalem, that great city, "where also our Lord was crucified" *(Revelation 11:8)*. And he will be joined by hideous creatures, like locusts, with the stinging power of scorpions, to torment the unredeemed people of earth.

> *"And in those days shall men seek death, and shall not find it; and shall desire to die, and death shall flee from them" (Revelation 9:6).*

Thus shall Isaiah's prophecy be realized that the "scornful men of Jerusalem" will have made a "covenant with death" and are "in agreement with hell." In performing this ungodly sex generative ritual, the Jew— and the Mason—will be joining in a "covenant" and an agreement with hell. God have mercy on their souls.

SEVEN

Straight Out of Babylon, Egypt, India, and Greece

The Incredible Sex Gods and Goddesses of the Jewish Religion

"...Hokhmah, the Father (god), and Binah, the Mother (goddess) sexually united and lighted up each other. The mother conceived and gave birth to the Son. Through the birth of the Son, the Mother and Father found perfection. This led to the completion of everything and the inclusion of all (four deities)—Father, Mother, Son, and Daughter. This doctrine elevates human sexuality ‹ ¹ⁱvine principle and humanizes God."
> —David S. Ariel
> *Kabbalah: The Mystic Quest in Judaism*

"For there is one God, anu   ·diator between God and men, the man Christ Jesus."
> — *I Timothy* .

Hey, wanna be a member of a sex cult? W   what about joining the Mormon (LDS) Church? Theiᵣ doctrine promises men that if they are faithful to founder Joseph Smith's message, they can end up as god of their own planet, supplied with untold numbers of celestial wives. Smith himself, historians say had some 36 wives—and that was just here on earth. Think of how many he might have somewhere up in space, as potentate of his very own planet.

Having for years studied the cult and religion of Mormonism, founded by con man promoter Joseph Smith and his lustful sidekicks in the little town of Nauvoo, Illinois in 1831, I would not personally advise a man to join this ridiculous "Church," but, regrettably, millions have joined. The twin promises of unlimited sexual pleasures and ascendance to the divine throne of one's own planetary kingdom seem to be irresistible lures to many.

Personally, as a Christian, I am very satisfied with my one wife, Wanda, to whom I have been pleasantly wed now for almost four decades. But as a student of false religions and cults, I have always been interested in uncovering the strange and bizarre doctrines and teachings of what I call the "Sex Cults and Religions."

Mormonism and Masonry—Twin Sex Cults

Mormonism is one such religion, and the sex angle in its doctrinal tenets is actually one reason this spiritual group is one of the fastest growing religions in the world, with reportedly some fifteen million members. Mormonism is closely connected to another religious cult, Freemasonry, and, in fact Joseph Smith and all of the LDS Church's earliest founders were Freemasons.

Masonry, too, is a fertility sex cult. The Brotherhood's common logo, the Masonic square and compass, is a sex symbol indicating the sexual union of man (above) and woman (below). The "G" within the symbol stands for Geometry, Gnosis, the Generative act, Gaia (the Feminine Principle) and God (Unfortunately the Mason's "God" is Lucifer, given by the Brotherhood of Masons the cryptic name, "Grand Architect of the Universe"). The Generative act, of course, is a code phrase for sexual intercourse, and every one of the cult's thirty-three rituals is permeated with sexual meaning.

Judaism A Sex Cult

But if a man, or woman for that matter, truly wants to be in a fast growth, sex based religious cult, for the biggest bang (pardon the pun), I recommend *Judaism*. Yes, Judaism. It is the most intricate and esoterically decorated of all the many sexual cults and religious.

The Talmud and Sexual Deviancy

The Talmud is the basis for the Jews' emphasis on sexual deviance and on their craving for material gains and pleasures. The Talmud, for example, permits sex between adults and children. The male child must be at least nine years of age, the female only three. Jewish rabbis, businessmen, and high-ranking political figures in Israel are infamous for pedophilia, for world sex trafficking, and for sexual harassment of female employees. Meanwhile, Jews are at the forefront of the global pornography industry.

In the scholarly magazine, *The Jewish Quarterly*, Winter 2004), Jewish Professor Nathan Abrams examines the leading role of Jews in pornography. He writes:

"Jews play a disproportionate role throughout the adult film industry in America... Jews have helped transform a fringe subculture into what has become a primary constituent of Americana. Though Jews make up only two percent of the American population, they have been prominent in pornography."

Abrams says that there is a continuing hatred in the Jewish community against Gentiles and especially against Christian morality. This hatred drives the Jews to aggressively pursue the notorious pornography industry:

"Al Goldstein, the publisher of *Screw* magazine, said, 'The only reason that Jews are in pornography is that we think Christ sucks...' Pornography thus becomes a way of defiling Christian culture and, as it penetrates to the very heart of the American mainstream, its subversive character becomes more charged...

"Extending the subversive thesis, Jewish involvement in the X-rated industry can be seen as a proverbial two fingers to the entire WASP (white, Gentile) establishment in America."

According to Dr. Abrams, the Jewish domination of the sex industry is a stunning achievement worthy of mention. He approves this perversity, pointing out that Jews are proud to "destroy Gentile morals."

Now the average Gentile, even the ordinary Jew on the street, knows very little about the bizarre sexual rites, practices, and teaching of the Jews. But even the most basic students of Kabbalah are tuned in to the truly diverse sexuality of the Judaic religion. Some of the more politically correct rabbis will deny it, but they know what's going on. The Orthodox rabbis, especially the Ultra-Orthodox like the Chabad, the Hasidic devotees, the Lubavitchers, are reportedly deep into this sex magick. But even the Orthodox Jews who refrain from the Kabbalah's guidance well know that the 613 laws of the Halakhah (Jewish Law) are saturated with sexual shibboleth.

Talmud Jam-Packed With Sexual Instruction

The Talmud, the most holy book of Judaism, is jam-packed with fleshly maxims and doctrinal advice giving Jews permission to "enjoy" incest with minor children, fornicate with the dead (necrophilia) and commit gross acts of adultery with the neighbor's beautiful Gentile wife or daughter.

Why, in one passage, the Talmud glowingly speaks of a rabbi who had sex with every prostitute on the face of planet earth. You fornicators out there will be pleased to know that this very sexually active rabbi, according to the Talmud, will receive his "portion" in the wonderful world to come.

Having studied for over a quarter of a century the mythologies of the Greeks and Romans, I am well aware of the incredible fantasy sex lives of the mythological deities. Zeus, Athena, Venus, Hercules, Orpheus, Atlas, Prometheus, Mylitta, Europa, Poseidon, Iris, Hermes, Aphrodite, Oedipus, Minerva, Pandora, et al. The entire pantheon of gods and goddesses perpetually stayed sexually active, abducting, raping, molesting, and otherwise having all manner of "normal" and deviant sex with each other. They did it everywhere, too, in the clouds, in other worldly netherlands, in the valleys, in caves, atop mountains, and in the deep oceans. There was incest, fratricide, infanticide, and all kinds of notoriously wicked conduct among the gods and goddesses, generating countless instances of vendettas, revenge, and violence.

Babylonian Religion Similar to Judaism

The same can be said for the gods and goddesses of all the ancient pagan and Mystery religions, including those of China, the Americas, the

Pacific islands, in the Mediterranean, the Middle East, in North Africa, India, Persia and Egypt.

In ancient Babylon and the Chaldees we find a multitude of deities, many of a sexual nature. According to famed 19th century historian, Anglican Bishop Alexander Hislop, in his classic text, *The Two Babylons*, the Sumarians, Chaldeans, and Babylonians during one key period worshipped a Trinity of Father, Mother, and Son. The reigning human Monarch and his mate took on the character of these deities. King Nimrod and Queen Semiramis ruled as divine beings, but when Nimrod was murdered, his Queen, Semiramis, married their son, claiming that the spirit of the dead monarch had possessed the son. The Father was said to be "God" reigning in heaven.

Though this Trinity became most prominent, there were multiple gods and goddesses in the Babylonian

The Fish God was one of the Babylonian deities. The Jews claim today as their god and messiah Leviathan, the great serpent and beast from the sea.

Mystery religions, and people often worshipped one or another depending on what advantage they sought. There were separate gods that promised the faithful prosperity; some offered fertility to women; others were warrior gods, and goddesses, or deities promising health, long life, or other tangible benefits.

In Babylon as in Egypt, Greece, Rome, and India among the Hindus, seductive priestesses offered their spiritual and sexual favors to men as "holy acts" of deviation to the Great Goddess. By joining in sex with the Temple or Shrine prostitute, the worshipper was thought to be joining himself with the invisible Goddess. Intercourse with the priestess was a ritual with prayer offered before the act and a devout, colorful, salacious dance was performed by the priestess. After consummation, the man gave an agreed-upon in advance "gift" to the shrine or temple as an act of devotion.

Now these practices were common in Babylon during the 70 years of captivity (609-538 BC) in which the population of Israel was subject to Babylonian masters. The prophet Jeremiah had publicly stated that the Israelites and their religious and political leaders had already proven their wickedness back in Jerusalem. These abominations, in fact, had brought about their captivity in Babylon, after that nation's King Nebuchadnezzar conquered Israel and its capitol. While in Babylon these seven long decades, the religious leaders, instead of repenting for their gross sins, multiplied them by observing the demonic practices of the Babylonians and integrating them into their own dark closet full of spiritual treachery.

Upon their eventual return to Jerusalem, many of these wicked priests of Israel, along with the Sanhedrin, prided themselves on their learned knowledge of Babylonian Mystery teachings and ritual practices. Moreover, their "Oral Traditions" reflected their adoption of Babylonian magic, astrology, and other black arts. The Oral Traditions were set down in ink, becoming the 63 volumes of the Babylonian Talmud that is considered to this day by the chief rabbis to be Israel's most holy and sacred book.

The Kabbalah and Its Witchcraft and Sorcery

Later, in the Middle Ages, still more Babylonianism was melded together with medieval witchcraft and sorcery, primarily the work of Spanish Jew, Moses de Leon, and the Kabbalah became yet another system important to the rabbinical cult of "Judaism." Now, as we move boldly into the twenty-first century, the Kabbalah is at center stage. Its magical arts are adored by Orthodox Jews and other, less rigid Jewish religious groups alike. The Conservatives and Reform Jews, even the secularists are "into" Kabbalah.

Many Gentiles, too, are fascinated by Kabbalah, and they are often not discouraged by the rabbis. Kabbalistic rabbis delight in presenting their magical, pagan concepts at seminars, workshops, online, and in books, videos, and other methods to throngs hungry for these teachings. As with the ancient Mystery religions, the lure of sexual pleasures is one big draw, but the rabbis also promise that study of the Kabbalah will bring one happiness, bliss, physical healing and prosperity.

An added inducement is that the Kabbalist initiate need not pay particular heed to the rigorous 613 laws of the Talmudic Halakhah. The rabbis often do not discard but do downplay the Talmud in teaching the mysteries of Kabbalah to new recruits; they emphasize instead the carnal delights to be attracted by practice of Kabbalistic sex, meditation, chanting, music, etc.

Kabbalah Teaches That Judaism Has Many Deities

One thing the kabbalist initiate discovers is that Judaism, thanks to the Kabbalah, is a polytheistic religion with its universe populated by numerous sex gods and goddesses. Jehovah, or "I AM," the God of the Torah and Old Testament is all but forgotten in the crush to learn the new theology of the many sexually promiscuous deities. Much of the activity of the devoutly religious goes toward inducing and encouraging these many deities to copulate with each other. Sex is thought to create positive energy forces and "create" prosperity, etc.

The pantheon of gods and goddesses in esoteric Judaism and their various roles is not easily understood, but acclaimed Professor Israel Shahak of Hebrew University in Jerusalem took a stab at it in his excellent book, *Jewish History, Jewish Religion: The Weight of Three Thousand Years*. Here is just a part of his description of the Kabbalist system:

"According to the cabbala, the universe is ruled not by one god but by several deities, of various characters and influences, emanated by a dim, distant First Cause. Omitting many details, one can summarize the system as follows. From the First Cause, first a male god called 'Wisdom' or 'Father' and then a female goddess called 'Knowledge' or 'Mother' were emanated or born. From the marriage of these two, a pair of younger gods were born: Son, also called by many other names such as 'Small Face' or 'The Holy Blessed One'; and Daughter, also called 'Lady' (or 'Matronit', a word derived from Latin), 'Shekinah', 'Queen', and so on.

"These two younger gods should be united, but their union is prevented by the machinations of Satan, who in this system is a very important and independent personage.

"The Creation was undertaken by the First Cause in order to allow them to unite, but because of the Fall they became more disunited than ever, and indeed Satan has managed to come very close to the divine daughter and even to rape her (either seemingly or in fact—opinions differ on this).

"The creation of the Jewish people was undertaken in order to mend the break caused by Adam and Eve, and under Mount Sinai this was for a moment achieved: the male god Son, incarnated in Moses, was united with the goddess, Shekinah. Unfortunately, the sin of the Golden Calf again caused disunity in the godhead; but the repentance of the Jewish people has mended matters to some extent.

"Similarly, each incident of biblical Jewish history is believed to be associated with the union or disunion of the divine pair. The Jewish conquest of Palestine from the Canaanites and the building of the first and second Temple are particularly propitious for their union, while the destruction of the Temples and exile of the Jews from the Holy Land are merely external signs not only of the divine disunion but also of a real 'whoring after strange gods': Daughter falls closely into the power of Satan, while Son takes various female satanic personages to his bed, instead of his proper wife."

Professor Shahak emphasizes that Judaism is far removed from the simple religion given by God to Moses and the prophets. It is, he relates, a polytheistic religion of many different gods and goddesses, some quite vulgar and vain. He adds:

"Whatever can be said about this cabbalistic system, it cannot be regarded as monotheistic, unless one is also prepared to regard Hinduism, the late Graeco-Roman religion, or even the religion of ancient Egypt, as 'monotheistic.'"

Even with all these many deities, Shahak explains, the Kabbalah Jews also tack on "Satan," whom they pray to and accord recognition.

Shekinah, the Mother of Israel

Athal Bloomer, a previously practicing Jew who writes under the name

"Ahron Yosef," says that the Shekinah, the Mother, is the central concept of Judaic mysticism. The Shekinah is known as the Divine (or real) presence. Of course, the title or name "Shekinah" is not found anywhere in the Holy Bible, but many Jews insist that the holy cloud that followed and overshadowed the Children of Israel in the wilderness for forty years after they escaped the captivity of Pharaoic Egypt was the "Shekinah" glory. This mother goddess is known by the Jews under many titles—as the Queen of Heaven, as mother of Israel, Sabbath Queen, Matronita (Mataar) a warrior queen who fights against the enemies of Israel, the Feminine Wisdom, the Holy Virgin, the Earth Virgin, the Virgin of Jerusalem, or simply as the "Community of Israel." She is also depicted as the feminine version of Leviathan the Serpent.

Daniel Matt, author of *Zohar—The Book of Enlightment,* explains that titles such as the Sabbath Queen and the *Shekinah* are one and the same. Jewish witches today worship her as the Earth Mother. Malkuth is taught as the name of the lower Mother aspect (Yes, there is a higher and a lower mother as is often the case in an occult system in which the concept of "As Above, So Below" and the conflict of opposites is found).

The Prophet Jeremiah fiercely condemned Israel's adoration of this very same feminine deity, whom the apostate Israelites worshipped as the "Queen of Heaven:"

"Seest thou not what they do in the cities of Judah and in the streets of Jerusalem?

"The children gather wood, and the fathers kindle the fire, and the women knead *their* dough, to make cakes to the queen of heaven, and to pour out drink offerings unto other gods, that they may provoke me to anger.

"Do they provoke me to anger? saith the LORD: *do they* not *provoke* themselves to the confusion of their own faces?

"Therefore thus saith the Lord GOD; Behold, mine anger and my fury shall be poured out upon this place, upon man, and upon beast, and upon the trees of the field, and upon the fruit of the ground; and it shall burn, and shall not be quenched."

A Confusion of Deities and Sexual Activities

In the Kabbalah teachings, this Mother, named Binah, has constant, never ending sex (union) with the Father, Hokhmah, and this is a perpetually creative—that is, a *generative* act. In one of her several forms, however, the goddess is *Malkuth*, the Daughter (who is also Sister) and there is the Son, *Tif'eret*. They all have holy sex together by the Son's use of the *Yesod* (also called *Hesod* or *Jesod*), the penis, which is one of the ten Sephiroth (*Sefirot*) deities or manifestations (some say "attributes," "expressions," or "aspects") of the Supreme Deity, whom the Jews call "Ein Sof." All ten of the sephiroths are gods or goddesses and together they make up the whole Deity. The first nine Sefirots are in turn divided into three triads, each containing three sefirot (deities). The tenth sefirot is the Shekinah. So special and honored is this tenth Sefirot that she is not part of the three triads. As I stated, her name in the Sephiroth (Tree of Life) is "Malkuth."

Now the lowest triad of sefirots on the kabbalistic Tree of Life is said to be the two legs, right and left, *Ein Sof*, the Supreme God, and his penis, or phallus. Each of the three has a name, and the phallus god is named "*Yesod*" (foundation). Yes, the penis is the very Foundation of the Jews' Supreme Father God. Moreover, according to the doctrine of Kabbalah, the light and power of the Sefirot (Tree of Life), the whole of the ten gods and goddesses, is channeled through the phallus god, Yesod, to the lowest, tenth deity, which is the Mother in her form of the Daughter, Malkuth. Thus, the divine light of the great God of the Jews is generated by the work of its phallus part.

In the Kabbalah, many secretive words are used to represent another thing. For example, reference is made to *"The Garden,"* which turns out to be a symbol for Malkuth's vagina between her thighs. The Son, Tif'eret, plants his Hesod, the phallus, inside the "Garden" of the Daughter.

Mention is also made of the *Bride* and her groom, the *Husband*. The Bride, of course, is Malkuth, the Daughter, and her Husband is the Son, Tif'eret. The Husband goes to the Garden where he has *union* with the Bride.

The Hebrew letter "VAV," assigned the number 6 in the Jewish gematria (numerology) is related to the Sefirot's (Tree of Life's) Son God.

In the classic textbook, *The Holy Kabbalah*, by Arthur Edward Waite, we learn that, "The Shekinah (the Mother/Goddess) is the president of a Mystery of Sex." The "Secret Doctrine of Kabbalah" is of sex, Waite adds: the God's penis is known as the "fount," and if he does not use it enough in sexual union with the feminine aspects, he is guilty of "an irreparable crime." The same is true for a Jewish man. If a man does not have sexual union often, he is not holy, for, Waite explains, "A man is sanctified at the moment of intercourse."

Thus, "The holy sex act is spiritual," and when engaged in coitus; that is, sexual union, a man receives the "Glory" in himself: "The Most Holy Shekinah on high cohabits and indwells during the external (sex) act."

"The two spirits (man and Shekinah/Mother) are interchanged," Waite says, as the man's phallus (penis) enters into the body of the woman. The two parties in copulation, are said to be neither male nor female, but have become a unified spiritual entity "composed of the world above." As Above, So Below.

According to Kabbalist authorities Dan and Lavinia Cohm-Sherook, the sex act provides and is the very "life force of the cosmos." They note that eroticism is rampant especially among the influential Hasidic Orthodox Jews and some of that sect's works. Movement during prayer is depicted as copulation with the Shekinah. Evidently, the satanic jerking back and forth and swaying of the Orthodox Jews at the so-called "Wailing Wall" in Jerusalem on the Temple Mount is also, for many, a sexual thing. The worshippers believe themselves to be having sexual intercourse with Malkuth or with the Shekinah.

This is the same teaching to be found in the Hindu religion. The very word *"yoga"* means to be *"yoked"* with the Goddess, known as the "Shakti." And it is the same in every Mystery religion since time immemorial, dating back to Babylon and Pharaoic Egypt.

In the Jewish religion; sex on the Sabbath is especially important. Waite says this "being the moment when the Holy One (the Son's phallus) is united to the "Community of Israel" (Daughter's vagina). In sexual union on the Sabbath, Jewish man becomes "one and perfect."

According to the Kabbalist doctrine, Waite reveals, "He (the male Jew) draws down the Holy Spirit upon him and he is called the Son of the Holy One, blessed be He."

"The Supreme Mystery is a Mystery of Sex," Waite explains, and the principle is that a man must be "attached" (sexually connected) to the female for the Shekinah to be with him. In effect, no sex, no blessing, no Mother Goddess within. And this deficiency is considered a very serious situation.

The Kabbalists stress that no man can enter the "true life" unless he joins in sex. "The worker in God's Vineyard" is he who has sex. A man cannot know God unless he enters the "Garden" and experiences what is called the "Real Presence" of the Mother (or Daughter) so *righteousness* is the fruit of intercourse.

The *Zohar* specifies that, "A man is completed and made perfect by holy union with a woman. Only he can make sacrifice."

Talmud and Kabbalah Agree

The Talmud is in agreement. Its teaching is that conjugal relations is a mitzvah, a "good work," and "every pleasure resulting from good work is Shekinah." The "Companion on high" needs Jewish men to do this good work so that divine creation can continue in the universe. Sexual union by Jewish men and women here on earth activates the spiritual environment in heaven and incites, or inspires the holy couples—the gods and goddesses—to unite sexually themselves. When the holy "Mother and Father, Son and Daughter are enjoying sex, Satan is forced to sit and wait. He cannot pester the already busy Goddess to have sex with him. The "Holy Family" having sex is the "Ideal Family," say Kabbalists.

Most important, only sex on earth by Jewish men and women is able to complete God. This is a heavy burden of responsibility for the individual Jew. The Jewish male must ever keep in mind this "divine principle" and always seek to unite with his wife. If not, God's powers are limited and weak. He, the male, must do the pleasurable work in the Garden for "Divine Generation" to occur. Only sex can result in the long hoped for *"Tikkun Olam"*—the mending of the world and the ushering in of the Jewish Utopia.

Waite says that the Kabbalah emphasizes the point here that "The pleasure which he (the male) experiences is meritorious work." It is holy. The Mother abides only with the male who has conjugal relations.

This principle is said to be "The Secret of Divine Generation" and is "reserved for the initiate." Evidently, intention and blood are keys, and so a Gentile gets no holy credit no matter how often he copulates. The Talmud says that Gentiles are *goyim* (cattle, or animals) and so their sexual union is not a spiritual act. Moreover, in the kabbalist theology, sexual intercourse is what produces *souls*. The Gentiles have no souls and thus have no part in the Heavenly Tree.

The Disgusting Sex of Kabbalah

David Ariel, a noted authority on Kabbalah, in *Kabbalah: The Mystic Quest in Judaism*, cautions that "All the Words of Torah hint at the divine Mystery;" in other words, at sexual regeneration. "We should not read the Torah literally as stories about human events but as mysterious and veiled hints about the inner workings of God and the relationship of the divine to the World...One searches out the hidden meaning."

In other words, we are to dismiss entirely what the scriptures actually say and go to the rabbinical "sages" for their illuminating explanations and fantastic fables.

Scholar Michael Hoffman II, in his incomparable, 1,101-page exposé of the Jew's dark religion, *Judaism Discovered*, comments that the rabbis invalidate and discard the straightforward words of the Torah and Old Testament and substitute for them their own, filth-stained myths and fantasies:

> "The message Satan has been whispering in the ears of those induced with the unclean Talmudic/Kabbalistic spirit...is that the written text of the Old Testament is not sufficient. It is incomplete and lacking.

> "Indeed, Judaism teaches that it is utterly incomprehensible and ultimately mute unless it is taught out of the mouth of the Talmudic rabbis...it is the rabbis and not the Bible, who are the source of all godly gnosis, wisdom, and holiness... The Talmud elucidates the core horror at the center of this heart of darkness by teaching that the falsification of scripture is central to understanding the scriptures..."

Hoffman proves point-by-point that the sinister rabbis, many easily shown to be ignorant idiots and worse, actually mock the scriptures, substituting the most base of satanic trash and nonsense—silly doctrines and fables that the world, in its politically correct paradigm, showers with honor and awards.

The Kabbalah is chief among this unintelligible garbage and is the basis for the most disgusting of fairy tales. It is filled with confused sexual exploits and a bushel basket full of psychological mumbo-jumbo that a hardcore LSD user or a lunatic might come up with. Yet, Hollywood stars and celebrities flock to the Kabbalist rabbis for "enlightenment."

"Like all Babylonian religions," Hoffman notes, "Judaism practices *magica sexualis* (sex magic)." But at a coarse, vulgar, and profane level typical of the most unlearned pagan peoples.

Sexual Codewords

The efforts of the rabbis to transform language to create a hidden interpretation is especially indicative of the gross transparent stupidity of these ridiculous men dressed in black, with straggly beards and serpent-like coils hanging from out of their little skull caps. Ariel, in his explanatory textbook on the Kabbalah's doctrines and principles, gives a number of examples illustrating how language, words and terms that we may take for granted are not necessarily the same when filtered through the guttural minds of the sex-crazed rabbis. To one of these wild-eyed religious scholars, a carrot is a penis, a door a vagina, a sky a bed, and a sea is wisdom.

For example, consider the following incantation or invocation, a common one in kabbalist ritual:"

"Hear, O Bride, Israel is coming! Prepare yourself! Your husband
is approaching in his adornments. He is ready for you."

The kabbalist reads and understands these words in a far different light than the unsuspecting and uninitiated person. The meaning for the student or master of Kabbalah: It is essential that the woman must get ready to have sex, that her husband has an erection and desires to have intercourse with her.

Now consider the following prayer, the opening passage of which all Jews know as the "Shema:"

"The Lord our God, the Lord is One. In one union, one devotion,
with no division. All the limbs are joined."

The kabbalist believes that by the sexual uniting of the Mother

In this ancient drawing, we find the high priests of the Jews worshiping the Divine Presence, the feminine aspect of God called the Shekinah. In today's Judaism the Jews continue to worship the Shekinah and some even have holy sex with her.

(Binah) and the Father *(Hokhmah)* or the Daughter *(Malkuth or Shekinah)* with the Son *(Tif'eret)* redemption is accomplished. The people of Israel, as is true of the Mother and Father, are redeemed through sexual intercourse and made one. Thus, we read that when "All the limbs are joined, and the *Hesod* (phallus) is inside the Mother or Daughter, the unity that is generated creates the one deity." Only then is God "completed." Only then can the Shema become reality and the words of the prayer, *"The Lord our God, the Lord is One,"* become reality. God is incomplete and scattered in his pants until man and woman engage in sexual intercourse!

Divine Sexual Intercourse of Multiple Deities

In sum, while Judaism pretends to be a monotheistic religion and while its common prayer refers to this monotheistic doctrine, in fact, as Professor Israel Shahak and thousands of other Judaic academic authorities and rabbis well know, Judaism is a polytheistic religion. Indeed, it is a polytheistic sex cult with divine sexual intercourse said to render redemption and generate holiness and righteousness. The "one devotion" of which the Jews speak is to the sex act, not to the One God.

Obviously, most of the rabbis simply lie about this, although perhaps a great number of them are personally convinced that their jumbled up, bizarre system of sexual rites and sexual energies on the part of numerous deities within the Kabbalah's Tree of Life, the Sephiroth, is a matter of One God carrying on a multiplicity of "inner workings."

One rabbi actually once tried to persuade me that the many sexual combinations of the Sephiroth (or Sefirot) "was much like a man masturbating"—in so doing, the rabbi explained, "the man's head, heart, hand, arm, and penis are all at work. These many parts," he added, "are all integrated into the One man."

Taken aback at the boldness of his metaphor and at its repulsive nature—suggesting that God's inner workings are similar to masturbation—I responded that a sane man, in doing such an act, does not assign names or a character deity to each of his body parts involved, nor does a sane man claim that masturbation is a divine, creative, redemptive, or salvidic act.

The next time you hear a Jew taunting a Christian, claiming that the Christian teaching of the Father, Son, and Holy Spirit is "polytheistic" and is a belief in "three gods," not one, you may want to recall what the Jews actually believe.

Violating the Ten Commandments

Though the *first* of the Ten Commandments given Moses and Israel commands that man have no God other than the One True God, the Jews have seen fit to violate this Commandment. As Jesus accused them of doing, they have substituted the Babylonian "traditions of man" for the divine guidelines given them by a loving and caring God.

Moreover, in embracing a theology of a humanized sexual "God" depending on men having sex with women here on earth to achieve his "completion" and their "redemption," the Jews are insulting and blaspheming God. What's more, they do so in the most vulgar and spiritually depraved manner possible. I pity these filthy teachers of debauchery on Judgment Day.

To imagine that, as David Ariel states, "Kabbalists created new rituals of redemption whose purpose is to bring about the resurrection of the Shekinah and her reunion with Tif'eret." What could be more blasphemous and spiritually sick than that? And then to conceal what they are doing with secret code words and kabbalistic Mystery language supposedly understood only by the *initiated*—what garbage! What pridefulness and conceit on their part.

In a fresh new version of the old adage, "sing while you work," Ariel speaks of popular hymns sung at synagogue and in Jewish homes that subtly refer to this "meritorious" work of sexual union. One classic hymn was that composed way back in 1560 by Shlomo Ha-Levi Alkabetz. It is entitled in Hebrew, *Lekhah Dodi*, or "Come My Beloved." This tune is said to be a Sabbath liturgy and its purpose is to inspire a "cosmic wedding celebration." In other words, join sex on earth and in the heavenlies, with the gods (and goddesses) and men and women participating. (And *they* say Judaism is an old, stodgy religion!)

America's Most Famous Rabbi a Kabbalah Sex Pervert

There is much evidence that some Jews actually practice their Holy Kabbalah sex ritual *at work*. Dr. Henry Makow, whose pivotal book, *Illuminati 2: Deceit and Seduction* exposes many of the methods, tactics, and practices of satanic Judaism, recounts the sexual hedonism of one of America's most famous rabbis, Rabbi Stephen Wise. Makow notes that Wise was a personal friend of both President Franklin D. Roosevelt and FDR's Jewish handler, Bernard Baruch. A Zionist advocate all his life, Wise died in 1949, and decades later the Public Broadcasting System (PBS) hailed him as "one of the greatest fighters for democracy and human rights of our generation."

Rabbi Stephen Wise blasphemed with his perverted sex acts.

Makow borrows from the account of Helen Lawrenson, who, as a 23-year reporter for the *Syracuse Journal*, in 1930 was sent to interview America's most famous rabbi. In her autobiography, *Stranger at the Party*, she tells what happened, and here are Makow's words relating the event:

"She made the mistake of saying she admired him: 'The next thing

I knew he had toppled me backward on the sofa and was making love to me…Before I knew what had hit me, it was over and not a split second too soon either, as someone was knocking at the door and calling his name.' 'My God!' cried Rabbi Wise, 'it's Rabbi Bienenfeld,' leaping and buttoning his fly. And so it was, not only the leading Syracuse rabbi, but with him was Mrs. Wise who fortunately did not have her hotel key.'

"Later, Wise lured her back to his room and forced her to her knees before him saying, 'Kneel before me in prayerful attitude, my darling.'

"Her worship did not include servicing him 'at that time' but she assumed 'he acted in the same way in every city he visited' and she wondered if he wasn't afraid of scandal. He replied that, 'every dynamic man had a powerful sex drive and should make the most of it.'

"Three years later, they crossed paths in the course of her work for *Vanity Fair* and she found herself 'on (her) back again, this time on the long table in his office, with Wise reciting in Hebrew, 'Lift up your heads oh ye gates; and be ye lifted up, ye everlasting doors; and the King of Glory shall come in'" Psalm 24:7-10 (45).

Makow goes on to note:

"Helen Lawrenson (1907-1982) was a good-hearted, literate, leftist dupe of the kind the Illuminati liked to have around (for obvious reasons). The point is she is completely credible. She became the Managing Editor of *Vanity Fair*, and the love and lifelong friend of both Conde Naste and Bernard Baruch. She and her husband, labor organizer Jack Lawrenson, were regular guests of Clare and Henry Luce. Her book was published by Random House in 1975."

This prayer after sex by Rabbi Wise Dr. Makow believes to be Sabbatian. The "King of Glory" is obviously the rabbi's penis. In fact, this is a prime example of kabbalist coded symbology. Kabbalism is permeated with Sabbatianism. Again, we see here the misuse of language to create a blasphemous context. The "King of Glory" is the penis; when the wicked and ribald Rabbi Wise commanded, "Lift up your heads oh ye gates" and spoke of the "everlasting doors" he was referring to his erection, to Helen Lawrenson's female genitalia, and the entering therein by sexual union.

His unreasonable yet meekly complied with order for the young woman to "Kneel before me in prayerful attitude, my darling," is indicative both of Wise's filthy and blasphemous attitude and of satanic confidence that he, the esteemed and much honored rabbi, was a Jewish god on earth performing a creative act of devotion to his gods, the Sephiroth. The stupidity and obedience of the star-struck young woman is mind-boggling. Well educated, she nevertheless had been inculcated into the Judaic cult—no doubt from the cradle—and believed that holy sex with this "great" rabbi was a religious duty and a "good meritorious work." That satanic forces of deceit were at work in this instance is undeniable.

Let me be blunt. The rabbis have built their fantastic religion around the working of an anthropomorphic Father God's phallus (Yesod). And that phallus is itself a god, and this phallus god connects (has divine intercourse) with a feminine goddess (Malkuth).

Jewish Fables

The Jews worship the genitals and consecrate the sex act (sexual union, or intercourse, i.e. coitus) as a creative/generative holy act by use of their genitals as instruments. Unashamedly, Rabbi Geoffrey W. Dennis, in *The Encyclopedia of Jewish Myth, Magic and Mysticism,* admits that the *Zohar,* the primary textbook of kabbalah, "includes multiple interpretations built around the concept of God's genitals." Is it any wonder that in the New Testament, the Apostle Paul described the religious doctrines of the Jews as "accursed" and as "witchcraft" *(Galatians 1, 3)*. What's more, Paul cautioned Christians to beware of "Jewish fables." The reprobates that bring such impure teachings, said Paul, are unholy:

"Neither give heed to fables and endless genealogies..." (I Timothy 1:4).

"But refuse profane and old wives' fables and exercise thyself rather unto godliness" (I Timothy 4:7).

"This witness is true. Wherefore rebuke them sharply, that they might be sound in the faith: Not giving heed to Jewish fables, and commandments of men, that turn from the truth" (Titus 1:13-14).

Those who bring such impure teachings, said Paul, "profess that they know God: but in works they deny him, being abominable and disobedient and unto every good work reprobate" *(Titus 1:15 and 16).*

"Even their mind and conscience is defiled," he added.

I am told that some Jews had no problem becoming ardent followers of Oregon's Rajneesh, Indian guru and his sex cult. The teachings of the Rajneesh were so similar to those of Kabbalah that some of his disciples addressed him as "Rabbi" and they spread a story that the Rajneesh was of Jewish heritage and bloodline.

Praying to Satan by Jews

Those who are the highest initiates of Kabbalah explain that many of the Talmud's onerous and time-consuming labors are accomplished to either entice the feminine goddess, Shekinah, or Malkuth, the daughter, to mate and have sex with her male god lover, Sefirot Tif'eret, the Son. It seems that, whereas this Son god, Tif'eret, is not eager to mount Malkuth and sexually unite with her, Satan, the Adversary, is constantly lurking about, pestering her and inviting her to enjoy sexual relations with him. Often, a Jew finds it necessary to pray to Satan, in the hope that this will divert him from pestering the Daughter for sex.

Professor Israel Shahak, of Hebrew University in Jerusalem explains the washing of hands as having a dual purpose, one to serve God, the other to appease Satan. He explains:

"Before and after a meal, a pious Jew ritually washes his hands, uttering a special blessing. On one of these occasions he is worshipping God, by promoting the divine union of Son and Daughter; but on the other he is worshipping Satan, who likes Jewish prayers and ritual acts so much that when he is offered a few of them it keeps him busy for a while and he forgets to pester the divine Daughter.

Indeed, the cabbalists believe that some of the sacrifices burnt in the Temple were intended for Satan. For example, the seventy bullocks sacrificed during the seven days of thee feast of Tabernacles were supposedly offered to Satan in his capacity as ruler of all the Gentiles."

Possibly this informs us as to why Jesus castigated the scribes of Judaism for this and similar practices *(Mark 7:5-8):*

"Then the Pharisees and scribes asked him, Why walk not thy disciples according to the tradition of the elders, but eat bread with unwashen hands? He answered and said unto them, Well hath Esaias prophesied of you hypocrites, as it is written, This people honoureth me with their lips, but their heart is far from me. Howbeit in vain do they worship me, teaching for doctrines the commandments of men. For laying aside the commandment of God, ye hold the tradition of men, as the washing of pots and cups: and many other such like things ye do."

What are we, as rational human beings to make of the extraordinary foolish teachings of the occult Kabbalist rabbis? Hoffman, in *Judaism Discovered*, expresses my own view when he incredulously asks, "how could a religious holy man, representative (supposedly) of one of the three great monotheistic religions, engage in sexual perversion under pious auspices?"

Sordid Teachings in Judaism

Hoffman notes how the Kabbalah and Talmud are both centered on a blatantly erotic interpretation of the Godhead. "The Judaic religion," he reports, "is built around a concept of God's genitals." In one mind-warping example of the folly of these rabbinical sex "geniuses," Hoffman explains how they use a phrase in the Old Testament book of *Isaiah* to demonstrate their utter depravity. *Isaiah 33:17* reads, "Behold the King in his beauty." According to the rabbis who gave us their much-ballyhooed *Zohar*, the Hebrew word *yofi*, "beauty," should be secretly interpreted as a euphemism for the *divine penis*. The rabbis also claim that God made man into a "divine image" by bestowing upon him the penis. The woman is inferior because she doesn't have one and so she is not anatomically correct. God has a penis. Man has one. Woman doesn't.

Hoffman also finds objectionable the secret teaching of Judaism that the mystic can find *redemption* through a heroic willingness to do evil. Immersion in the lowest of the low, in the theology of the Jews, is the path to redemption. They call it the "descent for the sake of the ascent." Thus, the fervent Jew embraces evil and engages in "holy sex" in a quest to achieve divinity, a self-deception. Again, Hoffman compares these sordid teachings to similar ones in the occult secret societies throughout history and today in such groups as Tantric (sexual) Hinduism and the Ordo Templi Orientis, or OTO.

In the past, many of these unseemly teachings were kept concealed from the Gentiles and even from many Jews. Today, the kabbalistic rabbis profit from establishing centers for instructing people hungry for this so-called "hidden knowledge." Sex-starved men and women have developed an unquenchable taste for Mystery and they line up before the rabbis to be instructed on the sexual appetites of men and women, and gods and goddesses.

Christians who have been duped into believing that Judaism either is "Christianity without Jesus" or "Old Testament religion" had best wake up. This is a horrid and monstrous filth devised by devils and sexual fiends. My advice is to run away—and run fast—when you see one of these workers of darkness—a Talmud/Kabbalistic rabbi. The title rabbi—in Hebrew, "master," fits these dirty-minded religionists to a tee. They are indeed masters—*satanic masters* of evil and deceit.

EIGHT

Riding the Serpent

"For this purpose the Son of God was manifested, that He might destroy the works of the devil."
— *I John 3:8*

Why were *you* born? What is your *purpose*? Many are intrigued at the prospect for knowing their purpose, the meaning of their existence. They buy books, listen to sermons, and contemplate, all in a quest to discover their purpose in life. But, this quest is misplaced.

Better, we should first seek to ascertain the purpose of the coming of our Lord and Saviour, Jesus Christ. Our own purpose is insignificant when we consider *why* Jesus Christ was manifested—His purpose for coming to this earth in the flesh, as God.

We can determine this purpose by reference to scripture. *I John 3:8* tells us that the Son of God became flesh for this purpose, *"that he might destroy the works of the devil."*

That "he might destroy the works of the devil." That was the mission of Jesus Christ, a mission that He carried out perfectly. The Saviour's final words on the cross signalled the completion of this great task, the fulfillment of His very purpose for being manifested in the flesh: *"It is finished."*

Jesus' purpose was to destroy the dominion of the devil and to conquer sin. In pronouncing the words, "It is finished," Jesus was announcing that His new Kingdom, a Spiritual Kingdom of light, had been inaugurated. This Spiritual Kingdom, made up of Christ's faithful servants, was to give His followers authority to trod over all the power of the enemy.

The Enemy: Prince of This World

That enemy is known as "the prince of this world," the "prince of the power of the air," and the "ruler of darkness." Satan, and Lucifer, is his name, the rebellious dark angel, said to be "god of this world."

> *"For we wrestle not against flesh and blood, but against*
> *principalities, against powers, against the rulers of darkness of this*
> *world, against spiritual wickedness in high places" (Ephesians 6:12).*

Yes, Satan is god of this world. And he is god of the "children of pride," both demons and humans who operate his dark kingdom, bringing temporary fame and fortune to some, but misery and misfortune to everyone who is not of Jesus' Spiritual Kingdom.

"It is Satan who is the god of our planet," asserted Helena Blavatsky, the Jewish mystic, in her demon-inspired textbook, *The Secret Doctrine.*

The scriptures tell us of Satan and of his fate. He is called the "great dragon" who was cast out of heaven. He is the one that "deceiveth the whole world."

> *"And the great dragon was cast out, that old serpent, called the Devil,*
> *and Satan, which deceiveth the whole world: he was cast out into*
> *earth, and his angels were cast out with him" (Revelation 12:9).*

The scriptures record that Satan, called the "Dragon, or the Serpent," is filled with wrath and brings great tribulation and suffering to the people of earth:

> *"Woe to the inhabiters of the earth and of the sea! for the devil is*
> *come down unto you, having great wrath, because he knoweth that he*
> *hath but a short time" (Revelation 12:12).*

The Serpent, angry at his certain knowledge of his soon-coming fate, goes forth in fury to make war with those *"which keep the commandments of God and have the testimony of Jesus Christ" (Revelation 12:17).*

All those who worship the Serpent inwardly hate God *(Proverbs*

8:36). Throughout history, evil men have venerated Satan as the Serpent of Wisdom. We find multiple instances in history. The Babylonians, the Egyptians, the Greeks, the Romans, the Chinese, the Aztecs, the Japanese and the Hindus of India all cast the Serpent as a holy being, a god who could take human shape at will, a god whose lust and greed brought intrigue and chaos to the world.

The Jews and the Serpent

From the days of Abraham, the Israelites, too, were deeply involved in this heinous devotion to the Serpent. Rabbis today praise the Serpent in the Garden of Eden. He it was who gave the gift of gnosis (knowledge) to Adam and Eve. The Serpent cunningly and subtly inspired Cain to slay his brother Abel, and then attempt to hide what he had done from the eyes of God.

The rod in Moses' hand magically changed and became the devouring Serpent of the serpents controlled by Pharaoh's high priests.

In *Genesis 49:17* we find it is the serpent, an adder, who, Jacob prophesied, would, in the guise of Dan, be head of one of the 12 tribes of Israel, bringing judgment to Israel in the last days.

Though the Serpent has played an important part in all the Mystery Religions of Antiquity leading to and beyond the Greco-Roman world when Zeus and Athena were represented by the slithering beast, it is the nation of Israel that has bested the entire world in its deification of the Serpent. From the days of Adam and Eve to this, the 21st century, we can trace a straight line of the Serpent slithering onward to be worshipped as the one, true God.

This trajectory is carried forth today by the Jews who, rightly, are called the *"People of the Serpent."*

The People of the Serpent

The People of the Serpent are themselves liars who have been deceived by the most clever liar of all time. This deception causes the Jews—though, thankfully, not all the Jews—*to ride the Holy Serpent* onward to their and its ultimate destiny. Their eyes are blinded and they cannot hear, so long has been their historic ride atop the beast of prophecy.

It was Moses, their law giver, who understood the great deception that would occur among the people of Israel in the last days. He understood the destiny that was to be theirs in bringing the slithering

Serpent to Jerusalem, and he cried out in agony to his tribe and nation:

> *"Gather unto me all the elders of your tribes, and your officers, that I may speak these words in their ears, and call heaven and earth to record against them. For I know that after my death ye will utterly corrupt yourselves, and turn aside from the way which I have commanded you; and evil will befall you in the latter days; because ye will do evil in the sight of the Lord, to provoke him to anger through the work of your hands." (Deuteronomy 31:28-29)*

It is the People of the Serpent whom we are studying and analyzing in this book. And it is their supreme being, Satan, in his disguise as the *Holy Serpent*, whom we find at the apex of the Israel nation. He is at the center of Judaism and the Kabbalah.

The veneration and worship by Jews of Satan, the Serpent, comes under several names. Apparently, the rabbis have sought to hide the identity of the one whom they secretly worship. Almost 200 years ago, the book *Kol Ha Tor—An Outline of Redemption* was published, authored by Rabbi Hillel Rivlin, disciple of the famous rabbinical authority, the Gaon of Vilna, Rabbi Eliyahu ben Shlomo Zalman. The *Kol Ha Tor* promises to reveal the secrets of the last days for the Jews, including their ultimate victory over the Gentiles, their acquisition of great wealth, and their ascension to world power.

Veiling the name Satan, the *Kol Ha Tor* puts forth the covert name *"Metatron"* as the force behind the coming Jewish rise to power. Metatron is said by the Kabbalah and *Kol Ha Tor* to be the Meta-archangel.

Rabbi Joel Bakst, in his book, *The Secret Doctrine of the Gaon of Vilna (Volume 1),* claims that Metatron is *"the collective Oversoul and collective guardian of the Nation of Israel."* He is the overseer of the people's redemption.

Bakst says that Metatron handles the "serpentine path of planetary transformation."

The *Kol Ha Tor* seems to promote Metatron, Leviathan, and the Holy Serpent, as the keys to understanding the messianic role of redemption.

By whatever name he is called, unlike almost any religion and people that have ever existed, the Holy Serpent is greatly worshipped and adored by the Jews. He is, in fact, honored by the Jews in their Kabbalah as the

Metatron is said to be the angelic serpent who is the guide on the Jews' "serpentine path of planetary transformation." This is an artist depiction of the "holy redeemer."

Messiah of the Jews and as the Redeemer of the people of Israel.

The Ultimate Secret

This is the ultimate secret of the Jews. Moreover, their idolatrous worship of the Holy Serpent is a concealed and ineffable secret that would have forever remained shrouded in Mystery and fable were it not for this one fact: That Jesus Christ has issued this royal edict:

> *"Therefore whatsoever ye have spoken in darkness shall be heard in the light; and that which ye have spoken in the ear in closets shall be*

proclaimed upon the housetops" (Luke 12:3).

So, the secret mystery, the talmudic and kabbalistic worship of Satan, cleverly clothed as the dragon, the Holy Serpent, is revealed. What has been whispered in ears in private rooms for many centuries by the so-called "learned rabbis" is now shouted from the housetops.

The Jews are outed as miserable followers of Satan, as murderers of men, and as hateful deniers of Truth. Jesus is proven correct in His assertion to the Jews:

> *"Ye are of your father the devil, and the lusts of your father ye will do. He was a murderer from the beginning and abode not in the truth, because there is no truth in him" (John 8:44).*

NINE

The Dragon, The Serpent, and "Creative Destruction"

"And they worshipped the dragon which gave power unto the beast: and they worshipped the beast, saying, who is like unto the beast? Who is able to make war with him?"
— *Revelation 13:4*

In Revelation 13, we are informed of two beasts to arise and fulfill the last days prophecies. One of these beasts will rise up out of the sea; the other from the earth. Interestingly, Satan has no power of his own and must follow this script laid down by God in the book of Revelation.

Accordingly, in the Jewish religion are two beasts, or serpents. These two are of a humongous size. One is in the sea, the other in the wilderness—exactly as described in the New Testament's book of Revelation!

It is the dragon, Satan, which empowers the beast (the Serpent) to do his Great Work of *"creative destruction."* Byron L. Sherwin writes of the Great Work in his book, *Kabbalah: An Introduction to Jewish Mysticism:*

"Evil and catastrophe are endemic factors in the process of evolution. Without evil there could be no good, without destruction, creation could not take place."

As Henry Makow exposes in his excellent book, *Illuminati 3: Satanic Possession*, kabbalists believe the Christian Old Order must be ruthlessly destroyed before the Satanic New World Order can be built.

Freemasons—who practice a form of Judaism—call themselves, *The Builders*, and they boast of building a new world on the ashes of the old. Their 33rd degree motto is, *Order out of Chaos*.

Makow notes the Communists also "advocated the destruction of nation, religion, and family and the transfer of all private wealth to the Illuminati bankers, in guise of the state." The Communists were also Jews.

According to the Masons, as part of this ongoing chaos and destruction, the true God is to be banished and a new god, the unknowable Great Architect, is to be exalted.

Judaism and the Holy Serpent: Destructive Agents

Judaism, too, believes in this new god, whom the Kabbalah calls *Ein Sof*, the ineffable, distant unknowable deity. This deity sends forth sparks throughout the Tree of Life and sponsors war after war on earth until his chief agent, the Holy Serpent, delivers up the Kingdom to His Serpent People, the Jews.

The Jewish neocons who control America and are now implementing the New World Order realize that their historic mission is to invent wars and to destroy culture. By way of this "creative destruction," the neocons expect that Satan will be encouraged to establish his long sought for Kingdom on earth.

Michael Ledeen, a neocon who is a well-known U.S. intelligence and foreign policy operative, explains this historic mission of the kabbalistic Jews:

> "Creative destruction is our middle name, within our society and
> abroad. We tear down the Old Order every day, from business to
> science, literature, art, architecture, and cinema to politics and the
> law. Our enemies have always hated this whirlwind of energy and
> creativity which menaces their traditions (whatever they may be)
> and shames them for their inability to keep pace... We must
> destroy them to advance our historic mission."

The neocon Jews drew the first American blood of the 21st century in the 9/11 strike. They banded together, forming the *Project for a New American Century*. In a special report that soon became the basis for the foreign policy of the Bush-Cheney Administration, the neocons said that there needed to be an attack on America similar to Pearl Harbor. After such a shocking surprise attack, Americans could be easily marshaled to fight terrorists and governments around the globe. Thus would the military supremacy of America, chief ally of Zionist Israel, be established.

The 9/11 assaults took place shortly after this report was released, and the world situation has never been the same. The U.S. is continually seeking *Ordo Ab Chao* in the world. Michael Ledeen must be very proud. As we read in the *Protocols of the Learned Elders of Zion, (Protocol 13):* "Who will ever suspect then that all these people were stage-managed by us according to a political plan which no one has so much as guessed at in the course of many centuries."

Jews Use Creative Destruction to Become Gods and Create a New World

It was Jewish banker Otto Kahn who said the Jews will become "God." He wrote:

> "Our mission consists in promulgating the new law and in creating
> a God...by identifying it with the nation of Israel, which has
> become its own Messiah" (Comte de St. Aulaire, *Geneva versus
> Peace*, p.78).

The mission of the Jews is the building of a New World. *Tikkun Olam*, the "mending or repairing of the world," means that the Jews will use "creative destruction" to destroy the structures and cultures of this world, a process in which they are currently heavily engaged.

The making of a *New Reality* is the "historic mission" of the Jewish elite. It is this New Reality which is being fashioned today as the world is remade so that Satan will accomplish his objective of *As Above, So Below.*

It's the Dragon, Satan, who, the book of *Revelation* tells us, gives *power* to the beast to achieve his historic mission, this New Reality. It must, therefore, be the Dragon that has mated the Jewish beast, the Holy Serpent, with the world's greatest super power, the United States of America. That is why Bush and Cheney embraced the neocon's Project for a New American Century. The President must obey the *power* of the

Dragon. The almost supernatural power of U.S. military forces must be applied in the Middle East and throughout the world. Nation after nation must be destabilized until, finally, the whole world is in chaos.

Then, order can be restored, and on top of the ashes, the Serpent sits. He stirs. Arising from the embers of Chaos, the Phoenix flutters first, then flies homeward to victory. *Tikkun Olam* will have been achieved.

The Dragon Gives Power to the Jews

The Dragon has power to give his earthly throne to the Jews. Helena Blavatsky, often credited as the founder of the New Age Movement, herself a Jew, wrote:

> "He is called the Dragon of Wisdom… as all the Logos of all the ancient religions are connected with, and symbolized by serpents. In Old Egypt, the god Nahbkoon was represented as a Serpent on human legs… This symbol is identical with one which was called "the first of the celestial gods," the god Hermes, or Mercury with the Greeks, to which God Hermes Trismegistus attributed the invention of magic and the first initiation of men."

Helena Blavatsky even blasphemed "Christ," whom she said is not necessarily Jesus but can be any messiah figure, by portraying him also as a "dragon serpent." Christ, unlike Jesus, said Blavatsky, is the god and god-spirit in all the ancient Mystery religion systems. He is the "god" who initiated men into "magic" (witchcraft and black magic).

Revelation 12:9 reveals to us the actual identity of the one of whom Blavatsky speaks. It is the same "God" who, in the Kabbalah, is said to "enclose the universe inside him."

> *"And the great dragon was cast out, that old serpent, called the Devil, and Satan, which deceiveth the whole world: he was cast out into the earth, and his angels were cast out with him."*

So, we see that the Dragon, the Serpent, and Satan are one and the same Being. This Being is, moreover, the Messiah, or "Christ" of the Jews.

David Spangler, a Jew who is a top New Age leader, says he receives regular transmissions from "Christ, the Saviour," who he says is not

Jesus. Spangler's "Christ" appears to be the same personage worshipped by the followers of the Kabbalah. *Revelation 12:9* identifies him as Satan, who *"was cast out into the earth, and his angels were cast out with him."*

The Kabbalah speaks of certain divine "emanations" from Ein Sof, the cabbalistic false God of the Jews. These emanations include the ten deities from the Tree of Life—Kether, Binah, Hesod, Malkuth, and so forth. They also include a being who masquerades as "Shekinah," the goddess consort of Ein Sof whose Presence is said to envelop the earth. Are these kabbalistic deities, in fact, demon spirits, Satan's dark angels?

Spangler's Aspects of Divinity of God

Is this why Spangler, in his book, *Revelation: The Birth of a New Age*, wrote that he received this transmission?:

> "Am I god? Am I a Christ? Am I a Being come to you from the dwelling places of the infinite? I am all these things, yet more... I am the Presence which has been before the foundations of the Earth.
>
> "I am all those recognizable thought forms which you have formed of God and of Christ and of great Beings, but I am also more. I am aspects of Divinity of God which you have not learned to recognize but which will be revealed to you in this New Age."

This brings to mind the prophecy given us in the Book of *Daniel:*

> *"And the king (the Antichrist) shall do according to his will, and he shall exalt himself, and magnify himself above every god and shall speak marvelous things against the God of gods... Neither shall he regard the God of his fathers... But in his estate shall he honor the God of forces and a god whom his fathers knew not shall he worship"* *(Daniel 11:36-38).*

How amazing is this prophecy! The Jews today do *not* worship the God of their fathers. They reject the God who spoke to Abraham and to Isaac, and to Jacob. Instead, they worship a *"God of forces."* This false God is claimed to use his energy force to send "sparks of light" throughout

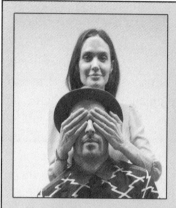

Top left: Angelia Jolie
Top right: Madonna
Left: Bill Clinton

Right: Mick Jagger
Below: Michael Jackson

Above: Paris Hilton
Left: Demi Moore

Right:
Leonardo
DiCaprio

These celebrities believe that wearing the red wristband of Kabbalah gives them magical powers and supernatural protection.

the universe. But he is mute. He cannot speak. Instead, he partially exists in emanations, beings, and elementals which Spangler called *"aspects of Divinity of God."*

Spangler's "Christ" transmission boasted that we have not yet learned to recognize these aspects but they "will be revealed to you" in this New Age.

Celebrity and World Figures Practice Kabbalah

Indeed, a great multitude of celebrities and world figures are clamoring today to study the "aspects of Divinity of God" as revealed by the Kabbalah teachers. The Kabbalah Center in Los Angeles has had a growing list of rich and famous clients. In this computer age, rabbis have numerous websites devoted to the teaching of Kabbalah.

Among the many Kabbalah students we find actresses and entertainers Demi Moore, Natalie Portman, Posh Spice, Madonna, Gwyneth Paltrow, Rihanna, Rosanne Barr, Ariana Grande, Paris Hilton, and Lady Gaga. Politicians include former House Speaker Newt Gingrich, former Senate Majority Leader Harry Reid, and former President Bill Clinton and Senator Hillary Clinton.

Teachers of Kabbalah are gaining fame among Messianic and evangelical Christians. Included in this category are bestselling Christian author Jonathan Cahn, author of *Harbinger*, and Messianic Pastor Mark Biltz. The Kabbalah and Talmud are both frequently quoted by Gentile pastors and evangelists who are "Judaizers," and terms like the "Shekinah glory" are often bandied about.

Books by promoters of these demonic religious systems take up a lot of space in religious bookstores, and Christian magazines flourish with the teachings of the Kabbalah. All in all, it is quite remarkable. This was prophesied in the Holy Bible where we find the Apostle Paul and others warning Christians of "Jewish fables" and of the bewitching "doctrines of devils" spread by Jewish teachers.

TEN

The Jewish Serpents and The Tree of Life

"And I stood upon the sand of sea, and saw a beast rise up out of the sea..."
— *Revelation 13:1*

"And I beheld another beast coming up out of the earth..."
— *Revelation 13:11*

In every pagan mystery religion, doctrine is formulated around worship of the *serpent*. The Ophites developed a unique worship of the Holy Serpent. The Egyptians had their cobra serpent on the headdresses of the priests, the Queen and the King. The Aztecs and Incas worshiped the serpent, Kulkulkan, and other snakes. The Hindus have their goddess figure, Kali, the death goddess whom the cobra represents.

In Judaism, the Serpent is celebrated because, say the rabbis, it was he who, through his teachings and actions, elevated the woman and man to the higher knowledge, the Gnosis. Through *Gnosis*, Adam and Eve were placed on the pathway to godhood.

The ancient Jewish rabbis and especially the authors of the Kabbalah's *Zohar*, have built what is today a very complex beast religious system, complete with two opposing Holy Serpents, one feminine, the other masculine. These two serpents, being phallic and vaginal idols, have sex together, in a generative process by which the Jews believe the world was initially created.

105

The Oroboros: The Serpentine Circle

Man's progress and the achievement of universal unity based on Jewish sovereignty over all, is contingent upon the success of these two serpents who, though opposites, are conceived of as existing unified as if in a revolving circle.

This circle has two half-life cycles. For each, a serpent presides. In a person's life journey, he or she commits both good and evil; eventually he ascends upward with the "good" serpent, emerging finally into the light and becoming the light. Upward, he or she progresses, ultimately attaining to self-godhood. The serpent is the one who helps the individual attain this godhood. He is, in fact, the helping *Messiah Serpent.*

The Kabbalah pictures this serpentine process as an *oroboros serpent,* also called a *dragon or worm,* biting its own tail. This, says Rex Hutchens, 33°, in the celebrated Masonic text, *A Bridge to Light,* represents God for the Masonic fraternity.

The oroboros, in the Judaic religion, represents the generative process *(ordo ab chao)* and eternity, i.e. the *Force.* This Force, this generative process, is "God." The oroboros is the Messiah of the Jews, the one who supernaturally will emerge from the pit, from the depths, and lift the Jewish people upward. Oroboros will launch the eternal Jews into the rarified state of *Deity.*

All these things are features of Jewish belief. The Jews believe they shall collectively be their own Messiah. The Holy Serpent will help them achieve this divinity.

They Will Be Their Own Messiah

In a letter published in *La Revue de Paris* (June 1, 1928, p. 574), and addressed to Karl Marx, Baruch Levy wrote:

"The Jewish people as a whole will be its own Messiah. It will attain dominion by the dissolution of other races, by the abolition of frontiers, the annihilation of monarchy, and by the establishment of a world republic in which the Jews everywhere excise the privilege of citizenship.

"In this New World Order, the Children of Israel will furnish all the leaders without encountering opposition. The Governments of the different peoples forming the world republic will fall without difficulty into the hands of the Jews. It will then be possible for Jewish rulers to abolish private property and everywhere to make use of the resources of the State.

"Thus will the promise of the Talmud be fulfilled in which it is said that when the Messianic time is come, the Jews will have all the property of the world in their hands."

Now, let us consider the first sentence in this revealing letter: *"The Jewish people as a whole shall be its own Messiah."*

Under what *"God"* shall the Jews operate, or serve, as their own Messiah? And by what laws, or *rulers*, shall the Jews rule their inferiors, the world's Gentiles?

The Kabbalah presents a strange Judaic God known as *"Ein Sof."* Ein Sof is a formless, mysterious deity unknowable to humans. Ein Sof cannot be prayed or talked to. This ineffable deity is unreachable by the divine Jews. However, Ein Sof does cast off sparks of light and emanations which become the numerous deities and entities found in the *Tree of Life.* Among these deities, each of whom in one way or another are directly worshipped by Jews, is the feminine *Malkuth*, or Moloch, and her phallic consort, *Hesod.*

Malkuth and Hesod are said to be avid and lustful sexual partners who are guided by the Holy Serpent toward the apex, the Crown of Life (Kether). The Holy Serpent is Metatron, or Leviathan. He also is accompanied on his slithering journey toward the Crown of Life (Kether) by *Shekinah,* female consort to Ein Sof.

This Shekinah, called by duped Christians the *"Shekinah Glory,"* shadows the female and male deities who collectively represent the Jewish people. She is the Presence.

Christians are often surprised to hear someone assert that Judaism has many minor deities plus a supreme "God" known as Ein Sof, and that this God has a wife, or mistress, called *Shekinah.* Tzvi Freeman of the Chabad sect of Judaizers, explains that prayers pass through Shekinah on to the unknowable Ein Sof:

"When we refer to G-d's presence within our world, then She is the *Shekinah*… In our prayers, we—all of us together as one—take the role of the Shekinah, petitioning the Holy One, blessed be He. In a way, God is speaking to Himself… We can't pray to Him as He is the Shekinah because it's His Shekinah that is doing the Praying."

In other words, all of the Jews in the world constitute the Shekinah Goddess! And when a Jewish man and woman have sex, they believe they yoke themselves with Shekinah and that, mystically, Ein Sof also enjoys this sexual relation: *As Above, So Below.* Freeman writes: "In many prayer books you will find instructions to say… 'For the sake of the (sexual) union of the Holy One, Blessed be He, and His Shekinah, in the name of all of Israel.'"

Equilibrium is the Goal

The cyclical generative process continues with sexual activity by men and women on earth with and for the minor and major deities of Judaism until harmony and equilibrium is achieved.

The Messianic Age will culminate when the Jews progress through successive generations of "order and chaos" until occult liberty is attained. The Masons know this as *equilibrium*, the supreme balance, when good and evil balanced together are in harmony. The Jewish religion harbors a belief in reincarnation (transmigration) and karma.

Jews believe they will not enter into hell, but all shall eventually progress to this Messianic Age when occult liberty becomes reality. This is the time of the fabled *"Jewish Utopia."*

As Nietzsche said, the age of the "Super Men" will arrive. The Jews will be the conscious God-Men. They will enjoy a Utopian paradisiacal life on a New Earth, over which they will preside as gods, as "divine sparks" of Ein Sof.

Utopia to Bring a New Reality

Billy Phillips, teacher at *kabbalahstudent.com*, says these "facts" are discovered in the *Zohar*, a prime book of the Kabbalah. The Zohar teaches that:

"…when the New Reality arrives our planet will change its physical dimension, enlarging… The borders of the land of Israel will extend and include the entire planet and all its people."

However, Phillips notes that, "The Messiah arrives only when individual people (the Jews) achieve a personal state of Messiah within themselves. Once a critical mass and specific threshold of people attain this personal, individual state, only then will the global messiah appear as a seal and not a savior."

"The Messiah," Phillips emphasizes," is a seal that confirms that we, the people, have achieved true transformation of our own nature."

"Only then," he stresses, "can we, as the collective divine being, or Messiah, turn the planet."

"After this state of Messiah is achieved, there will be one thousand years of paradise on earth, according to Kabbalah... That is the true Super Earth."

The Mark, Name, and Number of the Beast

Yes, the Kabbalah tells us that the god-like Jews will receive a "seal" confirming their conformity to the Judaic Messiah. What will this seal be? No doubt this will be the seal prophesied by Jesus Christ in Revelation 13, the *mark, name, or number of the Beast!*

This will bring to pass a counterfeit thousand year millennium of the Beast, thought by the Jews to be their Messiah and champion, the Holy Serpent. They believe this will be the Utopia, paradise on earth, but in fact, it will be the hellish era in which the Beast of Prophecy reigns.

The Jews foolishly think they will be their own Messiah. Oh, how intelligent and god-like they conceive themselves to be. Fools! Do they not realize there is a real God in Heaven and not an unknowable, uncommunicative entity called "Ein Sof?"

And do the Jews not foresee that their overshadowing Messiah, the Holy Serpent Leviathan, and the combined false deity of Malkuth and Hesod represent not the Jews themselves but the Beast with the prophetic number 666 *(Revelation 13)*?

The Jews actually teach in their Kabbalah's *Zohar* that the number 666 is not an unholy number but is instead, for Judaism, an exalted and befitting gematria number for Messiah. Rabbi Moses Hayesod, cited in the Vilna Goan commentary of the Zohar, happily admits this. He states, *"The number 666 contains within it exalted and lofty messianic potential."*

Tragically, we can see the ultimate destiny of the Jews. Deceived by the Holy Serpent, taking his seal and honoring his number, 666, as holy and exalted, they will be deceived, imagining themselves to be their own Messiah. They will thereafter join the Holy Serpent in the fire and brimstone of a tortuous hell. Utopia is not the prophetic destination for the Jews. Hell is.

ELEVEN

The Messianic Banquet—The Holy Serpent and The Great Purification

"May it be your will Lord our God and God of our forefathers…so may I merit in the coming year to dwell in the skin of Leviathan (the Holy Serpent) next year."
—Avraham Finkel
The Essence of the Holy Days:
Insight From the Jewish Sages,
(p. 99, 1993)

As prophetic events quicken in the Middle East and the Jews are becoming more confident that their "Golem," the United States, will continue to be their proxy in their drive for global domination, more and more rabbis are speaking out on the Serpent, Leviathan, and on the Kabbalah Plan.

Rabbi Geoff Dennis, professor of the Kabbalah and Rabbinical Literature in the Jewish Studies Program at the University of North Texas, is one who speaks of the Utopia, the "world to come." In an article entitled "Leviathan II—Demon of the Sea, Messianic Meal," he reveals how this topic is covered in the Talmud. He says that the Talmud uses two terms to describe the sea beast, Leviathan: *"slant serpent"* and *"torturous serpent."* Moreover these two are actually bisexual, which reflects the worldview of the rabbinical sages of the Talmud, *"who see the universe as permeated with male and female forces."*

113

"When the final rectification (end of all things, e.g. the last days) comes," writes Dennis, the Jews "will participate in perfecting the work of creation by literally 'consuming' the chaos...assimilating it into ourselves in a 'nutritious' manner."

The Feast of the Beast

In the Talmud (Baba Bathra 75a), we are informed about a great banquet. The Leviathan, having accomplished its Great Work and having elevated the Jew to the height of earthly power, will then "be slain and its flesh served as a feast to the righteous in the Time to Come, and its skin used to cover the tent where the banquet will take place:"

> "The Festival of Sukkot (Festival of Booths) therefore concludes with a prayer recited upon leaving the Sukkot (booth): 'May it be your will Lord our God and the God of our forefathers, that just as I have fulfilled and dwelt in this Sukkot, so may I merit in the coming year to dwell in the Sukkot of the skin of Leviathan next year in Jerusalem (Avraham Finkel, *The Essence of the Holy Days: Insight From the Jewish Sages*, p. 99, J. Aronson Publishers, 1993.)

How many Messianic Christians who observe the Holy Days of the Jews make this heinous prayer during the annual Festival of Booths?

This mysterious language of this prayer refers to the Jews' participating in the *Great Purification*, a bloody era of massive persecution of Gentiles by Jews and the death of most. The world must be "purified" of the filth and degradation caused by the inferior masses.

The Kabbalist notion is that after the Holy Serpent has helped the Jews seize the reins of the New World Order, that is, in Messianic times; the Jews will then "banquet upon the beast." They will consume Leviathan in a great feast. They will gorge on the flesh and blood of their victims. The Communist Jews in Soviet Russia gave us a glimmer of this murderous evil.

In the Talmud (Baba Batra 74b), we read:

> "The Blessed One will in time come to make a banquet for the righteous from the flesh of Leviathan...

"The Blessed One will, in time to come, make a tabernacle for the righteous from the skin of Leviathan... The rest of the Leviathan the Blessed Holy One places upon the walls of Jerusalem, and its splendor will shine from one end of the earth to the other; Walk at your Light, and be kings at the brightness of your rising."

The Leviathan beast, then, shines a great light on the righteous Jews. "He makes a light to shine after him," says the Talmud. Christians are told in Scripture that they are like "a light on a shining hill." Jesus told his disciples, "I am the light of the world." Now comes the Leviathan Serpent to mimic Christ and the Christian.

Notice that Dennis' article is entitled "Leviathan II—Demon of the Sea, Messianic Meal." In the Kabbalah, the Holy Serpent is man's helper because he "illuminates evil." Man's conduct in a lifetime is a combination of good and of evil mitzvahs (works). The Holy Serpent instructs man in the bad, creating the potential for the good. As in the Garden of Eden, the Holy Serpent is thought to have set Adam and Eve on the path to godhood. Jews believe the beast was the "helper" who aided man and woman in knowing right and wrong. He it was who gave the two "lights."

The Holy Serpent, in Rabbi Dennis' example, helps to bring "chaos" under control; thus he brings "Order out of Chaos."

Oroboros and The Force

Oroboros is another name for the sea beast, Leviathan, and pictures of the Oroboros serpent in a circle biting its tail are ubiquitous. The Oroboros is said to be *"a serpent of light residing in the heavens" (tokenrock.com/ explain—Oroboros).*

Oroboros is a Greek word meaning: tail devourer. This symbolizes the cyclical nature of the universe. It also symbolizes the *"creative destruction"* carried out by the Serpent in establishing equilibrium and order. It thus represents the fusion of opposites—the bringing together of "Order" and "Chaos." In all things Jewish, you find this dual meaning and the combining of opposites which creates energy. This energy is simply called "The Force" *(see Daniel 11).*

Kabbalistic Jews see the Oroboros as a wonderful symbol of their coming victory in the Messianic age, when the Jews become their own Messiah, stage their great Feast of the Holy Serpent, and punish those (the Gentiles) who have long resisted their coronation as men-kings.

Two Serpent Beasts

The Chabad, very fundamentalist, point to the significance of the Holy Serpent and its communion feast in a recent online article ("The Significance of the Feast of Moshiach," *chabadnj.org*, October 13, 2015). They say that the Leviathan sea monster "represents spirituality, which is hidden." The Chabad are highly religious Jews who separate themselves from this world to engage in strictly spiritual pursuits. The Tsadiq rabbi is an example, he spends much of his time studying the many volumes of Talmud and Kabbalah. The Chabad explains that there are actually two beasts, one from the sea, the other from the earth. The first is Leviathan, the second is named Behemoth. However, in the Judaic concept of As Above, So Below, the two are spiritually one.

"The second Leviathan beast represents the physical world and it is there, in the physical world where he is found," the Chabad tells us.

Obviously, left unsaid is the fact that this second serpent represents Jews who make money and use it for the good of Israel. These, too, are "righteous Jews."

"The righteous symbolized by the Leviathan reach superior levels of spirituality. However, the second type, who purify the physical, complete the purpose of creation, which is to refine the physical world."

Inspiration of the Holy Serpent

In the coming Messianic Age, the Holy Serpent will inspire those righteous Jews who refine the physical world. It is they who will take in all the wealth of the world; the Gentiles will hand this wealth over to the Jews. The righteous Jews will then "refine" the world by establishing a Global Government, which they shall lead, and they will make the rules by which men shall be governed. Christians will, under the Noahide Laws of Talmud, renounce Christ Jesus, or they will be beheaded. This, too, is the "refining" of the physical world.

Each type of Leviathan Jew is needed to usher in the Kingdom of the Jews: "When the redemption comes, the two classes of tzadikim (holy and righteous men) will influence one another, and each will absorb the special qualities of the other.

"In spirited terms," the Chabad teach "slaughter" means to elevate. This is the spiritual meaning of the "mutual slaughter" of these two beasts.

"Thus, through the combined efforts of the two types of tzadikim, the highest levels of spiritually will be drawn down into the physical world."

"The body of Leviathan, especially his eyes, possesses great illuminating power" writes Rabbi Eliezer in the Talmud (Shab. 77b). This illuminating power is the energy force behind the Illuminati, who draw on the Light of the Serpent to do their Great Work and complete Tikkun Olam (the mending and repair of the world.) This is why, in kabbalist drawings, the Holy Serpent is depicted as enveloping the world.

The Serpents Within the Serpent

Rabbi Bakst says that the Jews are at the very center of the universe inside the Holy Serpent's belly. The Jews, in fact, are called the "Serpents within the Serpent."

Placed in the Center of the Holy Serpent's circle, or ring of power, the Jew is said to be a god. Thus, Jewish scholar Eliezer Segal of the University of Calgary in Canada explains the function of the Ten Sefirot (sparks or emanations of Ein Sof, the unknowable "God" of the Jews) as the *"Pathway to Divinity" (blessedquietness.com/journal/housechu/shekina.htm).*

Sex creates the generative power needed to attain divinity. It is The Force which is generated when the "Shekinah," the feminine presence of Ein Sof in the everyday world, has sex relations, either with righteous Jews or with Ein Sof and the deities of the Tree of Life—the Sefirot.

In the book of *Revelation, Chapter 13*, we are told that the beast receives his power from the Dragon, Satan. In Judaism, this power seems to be based at least partially on the sexual power generated by the Shekinah glory, the female mate to Ein Sof. It is this feminine Goddess, who, the Kabbalah teaches, pervades our world. She is the *Great Mother* who energizes all inferior gods and goddesses. The New Testament identifies her as "Mystery Babylon the Great, Mother of Harlots" *(Revelation 17).*

The Creative Power of Sexual Energy

The Jewish Encyclopedia, using symbolic language, tells us that the human soul comes into the world as a result of sex by the Sefirot's Tiferet (masculine-son) in union with the Sefirot's Malkuth (the feminine daughter). These two lovers are inspired by the female Sefirot's Binah, in the upper region of light found in the Tree of Life.

Man has sex with woman and the *body* is born on earth. It is their spiritual duty to have sex and to procreate. In so doing they follow the example of the Son and Daughter Sefirot in the Tree of Life. Therefore sex between Jews is a holy and sacred act producing the sacred "Seed" and its end-product, a body.

The rabbis also believe that man can have sacred sex with the Shekinah Goddess *without need of a human partner.* Watching rabbis give messages on television, one notes the rocking motions, back and forth. Sometimes, this motion of the body can become quite rhythmic and persistent. This indicates that the individual is enjoying the "spiritual bliss" of sexual union with the Goddess, who usually is the Shekinah, but may also be the Sefirot's Binah or Malkuth.

Many of the Jews who go to the Wailing Wall in Jerusalem are "davening," rocking back and forth with their bodies and kissing the wall. They are actually having sexual relations with one of the Kabbalah feminine deities, most likely the Shekinah, the Divine Presence.

Here's the way *The Jewish Encyclopedia* uses euphemisms to describe this man-goddess sexual relation:

> "Devout worship, during which the soul is so exalted that it seems desirous of leaving the body *in order* to be united with its source, agitates the heavenly soul; that is, the Sefirot Binah. This stimulus occasions a secret movement among the Sefirot of all the worlds within the Tree of Life, so that all approach more or less to their source until the full bliss of the Ein Sof reaches the last Sefirot, Malkuth, when all the worlds become conscious of a beneficial influence."

The Jewish Encyclopedia thus claims that the Jewish man simultaneously has sex with the entire universe, including Ein Sof. The sex act of man on earth *influences* the whole universe.

In any case, as Rabbi Segal argues, the Kabbalah and it's many gods and goddesses provide man an opportunity to achieve divinity. It is the *Pathway to Divinity* and is little different than the *tantric sex* of the Hindus.

Secret Fire of the Serpent

The mystical Jewish rabbis say that:

> "The serpent is a primordial force of energy...being the principle of creation. Because it sheds its skin, it is a symbol of regeneration and renewal... When controlled or mastered, it is seen as mastering a... regenerating force...from which creation came." *(hermetic.com/stavish/essays/secret-fire)*

The serpent's "Secret Fire" is said to be "directly linked to the sexual principle and it is the "sexual desire of humanity that acts as its basic drive and evolutionary force."

Again, we harken to the phallicism of the ancient Mystery religions, from which is derived the Jews' religion. Both the Talmud and the Kabbalah give undeniable evidence that Judaism is nothing less than a serpent-worshipping sex cult. It is not a holy religion, and Christians need to avoid its seductive wiles and its call to adore one race—the Jews.

TWELVE

Doublethink in Practice—The Two Dual Serpents of Judaism

"Woe unto them that call evil good, and good evil; that put darkness for light, and light for darkness…"
— *Isaiah 5:20*

"Purify your hearts, ye double minded."
— *James 4:8*

In a kabbalist system in which conflicting, yet cooperating, gods exist, of which each must be appeased and satisfied, the concept of *Truth* becomes malleable. Truth in such a system is dynamic and ever changing. It is susceptible to instant change. Reality is transformed according to the person's immediate goals. Morality must give way to one's immediate needs. What is today moral and right may be viewed as radically immoral tomorrow.

If, say, a person has a strong belief in traditional, heterosexual marriage, that belief may be discovered suddenly to be incorrect and the opposite view accepted, that of nontraditional, same sex marriage being moral and right. It depends on which deity of the Kabbalah is accessed and on the individual's predilection.

The concept of Truth, then, is relative, and definitive reality is seen as idiocy. The majority view is usually taken and the minority is seen as bordering on the insane—or else, is completely insane.

1984 and Doublethink

Kabbalism is wicked precisely because morality in a kabbalistic religion is so flexible, elastic and dynamic. In *1984*, George Orwell coined the word, *Doublethink*:

"Doublethink means the power of holding two contradictory beliefs in one's mind simultaneously and accepting both of them."

The person gifted with the kabbalistic facility of doublethink has little sense of guilt. Nothing done can really be assigned to the immoral category. Sin is unconscious though it be carried out in a highly conscious manner. In Orwell's explanation, "In a successful manipulation of the mind the person is no longer saying the opposite of what he thinks, but he thinks the opposite of what is true."

Thus, 2 + 2 can equal five, or "Slavery is Freedom." The individual submerged in Kabbalah has no sense of right and wrong here because he is free to accept whatever is proposed, even if, to another person his choice may be incorrect, or even insane. The kabbalist does not feel an awareness of the discrepancy between right and wrong choices.

> **"Doublethink means the power of holding two contradictory beliefs in one's mind simultaneously and accepting both of them."**
> **—George Orwell**
> **1984**

Convinced that torture will reveal the truth, the inquisitor may torture without guilt. The military prone man may bomb and kill believing that "Democracy" will result from a successful campaign of rendering death. This even though, objectively, torture can be proven not to be efficient, and there is little or no prospect of attaining Democracy as a result of a bombing and killing campaign.

Kabbalism Results in Psychopathy

Kabbalism results in men who are no longer human but have been rendered as living "things." They are dehumanized machines, non-men of lost piety willing to be instruments either of death or life, unaware of feelings of empathy, subject to barbarism.

In sum, the kabbalist is a psychopath without conscience, able to sin against self and others without pity, seeking only immediate gratification.

The kabbalist says we shall engage in *Tikkun Olam*. We must mend and repair the world, when, in reality, they are thinking, we must devastate and destroy this world. We must do evil to achieve good. For good and evil are flip sides of Deity. And Deity can only be achieved through a simultaneous doublethink process in which the individual is made to experience both good and evil. Both evil and good are *mitzvahs*, good works.

The Kabbalah teaches what the Gnostics call *dualism*, the worship of two opposite deities at the same time. Symbolically, fire and ice may be utilized by man simultaneously, so that light may emanate from the unknowable "God." This is the *secret doctrine* of Judaism, the fact that

Satan and God are both worshipped, each given his due. Since, in reality, the true God of the Holy Bible, Jesus Christ, is not loved but besmirched, scorned, and spitefully hated by the Jews, the Talmud and the Kabbalah created the fantasy of yet another higher "God" who must be recognized and idolized. That God is known as Ein Sof. That unknowable God, that indistinct and distant Being cannot be known directly, so an *energy* spark which emanated from Him (or Her) takes his place.

The Caduceus is ignorantly, yet widely, used today as a medical symbol. Its use dates back to the Grecian gods and goddesses and spiritually represents double-mindedness.

The Secret Doctrine: Lucifer is God

That energy spark, that emitter of light, is *Lucifer*, the *Holy Serpent* in the Jewish lexicon. He is the Jewish Messiah, the helper and teacher of the Jews, the guide who, in the kabbalist Tree of Life, rises from the abyss, from the pit, to ultimate glory. That ultimate glory is godhood for the individual Jew, collective sovereignty over the entire world, and mastery over his Gentile inferiors.

This is the secret doctrine, that Lucifer is "God" for the Jew. And this doctrine, however grotesque and even frightening it may be to the

Christian, is, said Mirabeau during the French Revolution, *"veritably the code of hell."*

The code of hell spurs the Jew on to global domination. It inspires and motivates him to privately demean and hate his fellow man, the Gentile, even as he claims to love the Brotherhood of Man. Being filled with Satanism, led by Lucifer, the Jew has fallen into the fast grip of the *Tempter*, the same personage who tempted Jesus Christ in the wilderness. Jesus rejected that temptation, he would have no part of the devil's dark world. The Jews, however, fell for the temptation. They are still falling.

Light and Darkness

Jesus sagely stated, "If therefore the light that is in thee be *darkness*, how great is that *darkness?" (Matthew 6:23)*

James, the brother of Jesus, went straight to the core of evil, the mechanics of the works of Secret Doctrine, when he warned that, "A *doubleminded* man is unstable in all his ways" *(James 1:8)*.

James further admonished, "purify your hearts, ye *doubleminded"* *(James 4:8)*.

The prophet told the people of ancient Israel, "Ye cannot serve *both* God and Baal" (Lucifer, or Satan). You cannot halt between *two* opinions, he stated. But the Jew rejects this advice; he serves both Baal and a false, unknowable "God," thinking he is thus protected, being covered in righteousness.

The Jews are "beguiled" by the Serpent. Hypnotized by the Tempter, deceived by contradictory rabbinic words. As Eve, in the Garden, confessed, "The serpent beguiled me, and I did eat" *(Genesis 3:4)*. The Jews are slaves but do not possess the ability to see and hear. *Galatians 4* explains that physical Israel is in willing *bondage* to Satan and has, consequently, been cast out of the Kingdom.

Boasting vainly of their own greatness, the Jews have fallen into a trap, a terrible snare; it is a horrible fate to voluntarily accept one's servitude while insisting one is free.

Dualism and Doublethink the Basis of All Evil

This code of hell, *doublethink* or *Gnostic dualism*, is the foundation of all evil. It is not only the underlying lie of the Jews, the doctrine undergirds and supports Darwin's theory of evolution; Easton's system theory; Communism and Marx's diabolical materialism, and Asia's Taoism philosophy. It is seen in the Hindus Maya (illusion), and the Persian deity, Zoraster's, *Zend-Aresta*.

It is, moreover, the primary means in Orwell's *1984* dystopia through which Big Brother and his power-mad cult of bureaucrats were able to keep humanity under their absolute control.

Today, everywhere, this Secret Doctrine is practiced and is successful. It is reflected wherever we find two false choices. The dichotomy of Republican and Democrat Parties in the United States is one example. The black and white checkered floor of the Masonic Lodge is yet another. Yet, as modern as this doctrine is, the implantation of the *Double Mind* in the human consciousness can be traced all the way back to the Garden of Eden. There, Adam and Eve were presented the right way: the path to a continual paradise. Then came the Serpent, subtle and deceitful in his words saying, *"Surely, hath God said..."*

Ah yes, the Tempter drew first Eve, then Adam, into his wicked snare. He it was who first implanted the Double Mind in his victims. And the world would never be the same.

In Freemasonry, a Jewish religious system which incorporates the Kabbalah in all its rituals and in its ideology, this concept of *doublethink* becomes paramount. So much so that *two opposing, yet integrally linked gods* are formulated, symbolized by the double-headed eagle. Pike writes, in his classic Masonic text, *Morals and Dogma*:

> "For the eternal law is that there is no light without shade, no
> beauty without ugliness, no white without black, for the absolute
> can only exist as two gods, darkness being necessary for light to
> serve as its foil..."

Thus, Pike states, the Mason's reason to worship both Lucifer and his shadow entity, the Great Architect, erroneously thought to be "God" by outsiders. To worship both Satan, or Lucifer, and his shadow, the Great Architect, simultaneously means the Mason must balance all things. For every action, there is an equal and opposite reaction. Who can say that one is good, the other evil? Both are necessary for the human engine to be motivated onward.

The Feminine and Masculine Serpents

The religious Jew codifies in the Talmud and in the books of Kabbalah—

the Zohar and others—this simultaneous worship of two demonic entities. Both are serpents, one is feminine, the other masculine. One is called Leviathan, the other Behemoth, or *Yahweh*. One comes up out of the sea, the other from out of the wilderness (see *Revelation 13*).

The religious Jew accommodates in his daily regimen and throughout his life both of these serpent entities. At any particular juncture in his life, his actions and behavior might comport with the *descending* serpent. Or, again, it might be aligned with the *ascending* serpent. He might even appease both serpents simultaneously in his behavior and actions.

A Jew male given to adultery may, for example, pray the holy *Shema* just prior to entering the woman's genital organ, then consummate the sexual act. He may believe he is diverting the descending serpent's attention from its continuous efforts in the spirit world to sexually violate the goddess' daughter. Thus, the sexual union, though it is, to an outside observer, corrupted and immoral, becomes in his view, proper and correct. He is helping the regenerative energy process through the sexual act and propelling the world forward toward *Tikkun Olam* and restoration.

Freemasonry a Judaic Cult

John Quincy Adams, our nation's sixth President and possibly its most intellectual, was a fierce opponent of Freemasonry. Perhaps he did not understand it as simply another system of Judaic religion, but he did know that the Jews were among the most dedicated of slavery proponents, which Adams saw as antithetical to the Christian spirit.

In Freemasonry, Adams also found this same anti-Christian spirit, which was claimed by the mason to make a man a "better man." In Masonry, said Adams, in an address to the people of Massachusetts, "I saw a code of Masonic legislation adapted to prostrate every principle of equal justice and to corrupt every sentiment of virtuous feeling in the soul of him who bound his allegiance to it." He further stated:

"I saw the practice of common honesty, the kindness of Christian
benevolence, even the absence of atrocious crimes; limited
exclusively by lawless oaths and barbarous penalties... I saw
slander organize into a secret widespread and affiliated agency... I
saw self-invoked implications of throats cut ear to ear, of hearts
and vitals torn out and cast off and hung on spires. I saw wine

drunk from a human skull with solemn invocation of all the sins of its owner upon the head of him who drank it."

Do these horrors, known to exist and be practiced far and wide among Freemasons, make a man a "better man?" Or is this a prime example of man's conscience being ripped apart and reconstructed in the satanic alchemical process of kabbalistic methodology?

What Do Masons Want?

The ultimate goal of these atrocious terrors in Masonic Judaism is known. It has been often stated by the Masonic and Jewish leadership. C. William Smith, 33°, in 1950 in the *New Age*, the official journal of Scottish Rite Freemasonry, wrote that the Deity's "plan is dedicated to the unification of all races, religions, and creeds." He explained, "This plan, dedicated to the new order of things, is to make all things new—a new nation, a new race, a new civilization, and a new religion, a nonsectarian religion."

In other words, it is a plan designed to bring about the New World Order of the Jews (*Tikkun Olam*), subordinating all other races, religious systems, and governments. Masonry is a psychic and theological drive to bring about this *"new order of things,"* though its Gentile membership may be confounded to discover its Judaic underpinnings. We read, in *The Jewish Tribune* (October. 28, 1927):

"Masonry is based on Judaism. Eliminate the teachings of Judaism and what is left?"

Vicomte Leon De Poncins, in *Freemasonry and the Vatican* (London, 1968) quotes a Parish Jewish publication, *La Verito Israelite*, regarding these Jewish fundamental beliefs:

"The spirit of Freemasonry is that of Judaism...its ideas are Judaic, its language is Judaic, its very organization, almost, is Judaic."

Masonry, then, is a cover for Judaism and its Kabbalah. It takes advantage of stupid, unassuming Gentiles who would otherwise avoid its Judaic nature. Masonry even claims to be a religion. But more than just *a* religion, it makes claims to being the *only* religion. As the *New Age* magazine (Feb. 19, 1918) asserted, "Masonry is more than *A* religion. Masonry *Is* religion... Masonry is the Mother Church."

How surprised all these Blue Lodge Masons (1°-3°) will be if and when the Jews attain global control. The duped disciples of Masonry—coming from the various, so-called *"sub-religions"* of Buddhism, Hinduism, Judaism, Islam, and yes, Christianity—having been deceitfully used, will be cast out. Most will be killed. Only the loyalists will maintain their positions in society. This only after they are carefully selected for their subservient acceptance.

The Great Religion of Today Will Be Ended

The great religions of today shall be ended. They fit, in Jewish terms, the very definition of *sectarianism*. They will be subsumed—swallowed up—in Judaic Talmudism based on elevated kabbalism.

Rabbi Martin Siegel explains:

> "We are in fact...entering a period of Jewish-Christian reconciliation in which the world will ultimately adhere to a form of Judaism and call it Christianity." (Mel Ziegler, editor, *Amen: The Diary of Rabbi Martin Siegel*, pp. 67-68)

This new Christianity is here, now. Notice, please, that Christian superstars—e.g. the Pope and his Cardinals, Pastors Rick Warren, John Hagee, Joel Osteen, and evangelists Billy Graham and Pat Robertson—do not attempt to evangelize the Jews. They accept that the Jews will be saved through the Old Covenant, not believing in Jesus. Most believe in the *New Christianity*, in which the Jews are God's Chosen, eternally blessed, superior to Gentiles, destined to rule over an earthly kingdom. They even believe that Gentiles *must* give (money, military armaments, etc.) to the Jews in order to be blessed themselves in carnal things.

What a set-up for *Tikkun Olam*, the scheme for Jewish world government and religious mastery over all humankind.

Tikkun Olam: World Government

To succeed, the Jewish goal of *Tikkun Olam* must see the whole world become a "Brotherhood." Only the Jews will stand out from and above this unity of brothers. Global integration through unbridled immigration is necessary. This is why the U.S.A. is today, a multicultural basket case, a paralyzed giant of 325 million people, sixty-two million of whom do not speak English. It is the reason deportations have virtually ceased.

The same is true for Europe, where millions of Moslem refugees have invaded, driven from their homes in Africa and the Middle East by American and Jewish inspired bombing and assaults and military attacks on civilians.

This ideal of universal immigration and the end of borders and nationalism is expressed as far back as the late 19th century. *The Jewish World* (Feb. 9, 1883), stated:

> "The great ideal of Judaism is that the whole world shall be imbued with Jewish teachings, and in a universal brotherhood of nations—a greater Judaism, in fact—all the separate races and religions shall disappear."

All races and religions shall disappear, of course, *except* the Jewish race and the Jewish religion (Talmudic Kabbalism). As in communism, which is a distinctively Jewish ideology, *"All animals are equal, but some animals are more equal than others"* (George Orwell, *Animal Farm*).

THIRTEEN

The Serpent's Burning Hatred

"The customs of the Jews are base and abominable and
owe their persistence to their depravity...toward other
people they feel only hate and enmity."
— Tacitus, Rome

There is in history the tale of the "Wandering Jew." It seems as though the Jews have gone from country to country for hundreds of years. They refuse to assimilate, refuse to mix with their host, and then seek to destroy that host. It has happened across the globe, in Babylon, Egypt, Rome, Greece, in Britain and in a hundred other nations. The Jews basically "wear out their welcome," as they turn to wicked business practices—they cheat the host nation's citizens. They are immoral and clannish, and they put on airs of superiority and show contempt for locals. In a word, the Jews are, on the whole, extremely cruel and obnoxious. Before too many years have passed, they are asked to leave, or else kicked out.

The Jew contains within his psyche an irrational hatred of his Gentile host. The Jews' most holy book, the Talmud, is filled with hateful imprecations against all Gentiles and especially against Christians. The Jew acts out the hatred expressed in his Talmud and commits vile, terrible acts.

The Jews are essentially parasites and this fact has become widespread among the nations in which they have resided. In 1948, many of the world's Jews migrated to Palestine, where they conquered the unarmed masses, doing much violence and terror. But most Jews refused to leave the nation where they resided, continuing their parasitic behavior.

Why Are Jews Filled With Hate?

Why do the Jews possess so much hatred for the often generous people in whose nations they reside? In Mullins' *New History of the Jews*, Eustace Mullins notes that, "The Jews regard the Gentile people as cattle in the field, to be slaughtered for harvest…and if he has contempt and hatred for the gentile cattle, he has even greater contempt for his own kind."

But his immediate victim is the ones outside his own tribe, the *goyim* (Gentiles), in front of him. Mullins writes, "The Jew, then, regards his Gentile host with terrible feelings of hatred, envy, and contempt."

"The fact is that the Jews were known only as destroyers in the ancient world. They produced no art, founded no dynasties, built no great cities, and alone of ancient peoples, had no talent for the finer things of civilized life."

Even today, though the Jews make pretensions that theirs is a Great Civilization, they well know that their one great talent is the getting of

Satan's horned head in stone, on a pubic building in Canada.

money and gold. In all other areas, they are inferior. Knowing this, the Jews psychologically disparage and hate the peoples who have proven their greatness—the people of Europe and America and of the ancient lands. The Jews especially chafe at the fact they had to depend on the Moslems (the Ottoman Empire), the Russians, the Germans, the British and the U.S.A.

The Jews Hatred for America

In modern times, it has been the United States which has favored the Jews and showered them with billions of dollars in aid and armaments. Without the U.S.A., Israel would have long ago been swallowed up by its enemies. How do the Jews show their appreciation? By seeding America with thousands of Sayanim (spies) who have stolen America's most precious military secrets. In 1967, Israel even intentionally attacked the U.S.S. Liberty ship in the Mediterranean, hoping to blame the deaths of dozens of its naval personnel and the ship's loss on Egypt.

For the Jews, even those that are born in the United States, the goal is always found in the question, *"What is best for Israel?"* There is little or no native patriotic spirit among the Jews. No love of the U.S.A. Amazingly, the Jews have their own military veterans organization in the U.S., and it exists only for American Jews who served in the Israeli Defense Forces. Rahm Emmanuel, Mayor of Chicago and former White House Chief of Staff in the Obama Administration, served not in the U.S. armed forces, but in the Israeli military. This is a common practice among the Jews and rarely, if ever, found among the Germans, Japanese, Italians, or others.

Indictments Against Jews in the Bible

Their obnoxious behavior and lack of allegiance has been the case throughout history. Paul, in *I Thessalonians 2:15*, says of the Jews, that they have, *"both killed the Lord Jesus and their own prophets, and have persecuted us, and they please not God, and are contrary to all men."*

That is an astounding indictment! Consider: Paul reveals that the Jews:
1. Killed the Lord Jesus…
2. Killed their own prophets…
3. Persecuted the Christian Church…
4. Pleased not God…and

5. Are contrary to all men.

Read these five horrible indictments. Are these not true of the Jews over the centuries? Are they not true this very day? Is this not the reason for their universal persecution?

Tacitus, the great Roman historian, wrote:

> "The customs of the Jews are base and abominable and owe their persistence to their depravity... Toward other people they feel only hate and enmity. As a race, they are prone to lust, among themselves, nothing is unlawful."

Favored by the Romans, the Jews thrived and prospered. Many became rich through their trafficking in gold. Yet, they despised their generous hosts. Jewish historian Joseph Kastein, in his *History of the Jews*, writes:

> "To the Jews, Rome constituted the quintessence of all that was odious and should be swept away from off the face of the earth. They hated Rome...with an inhuman hatred."

The Jews Hatred of Jesus

The Jews hated Jesus Christ with this same type of "inhuman hatred." What was at the root of this extreme hatred? Is it not true that Jesus spoke bluntly of their greed and lust for gold? He stated, *"Ye cannot serve God and Mammon" (Matthew 6:24)*. He also called the Jews, *"hypocrites"* and *"whited sepulchers full of dead men's bones and all uncleanness."* He told them they were *"full of iniquity."*

For this, the Bible records, *"the Jews sought to kill him."* A man guilty of no crimes, who simply told the truth. But so inflamed were the arrogant Jews that they sought to kill him—and eventually did so!

The Jews, wrongly believing themselves to be "gods" on earth, were evil beyond measure. Jesus said they were *"serpents"* and were murderers exactly like their father, Satan. Compare His strong words with the mealy-mouth cowards of today, the Judaizer preachers and evangelists who praise the Jews and proudly declare, "I am a Zionist." What a travesty!

Jesus Said the Jews Were "Vipers" and "Serpents"

Jesus identifies the Jews as *"vipers"* and *"serpents."* Could this harsh language be justified? Yes, it could, when we consider that the Jews have a long history of horrific crimes against humans, even against their own kind. J. Kitto, in *The Cyclopedia of Biblical Literature* (1895), says of the Jews:

> "Their altars smoked with human blood from the time of Abraham to the fall of the kingdom of Judah and Israel."

The Jewish Encyclopedia notes that at various times in their history, the Jews sacrificed their own children to Baal: "Human sacrifices were offered to YHWH as King or Counselor of the Nation."

In the Biblical book of *Amos* we read that the Jews of that prophet's era worshipped not God but Moloch, known also as the god Saturn. They willingly sacrificed their own children, roasting them in fires consecrated to this demon god, Moloch.

How can the Jews be so proud of their civilization and history with this long, tarnished record of inhuman, terrible atrocities. Could any but a *"Serpent People"* so willingly sacrifice their own children to Satan?

Moreover, throughout their history, authorities have discovered thousands of instances of the Jews having kidnapped and murdered Gentile children as human sacrifices. These types of monstrous murders are sanctioned in the Jewish Kabbalah's book of *Zohar* (*Tikkun Zohar*, Berdiwetsch Edition, p. 886).

Dr. Eric Bischoff, a well-known Jewish scholar who studied the rituals prescribed in the *Zohar*, writes:

> "There is a commandment pertaining to the killing of strangers, who are like beasts. This killing has to be done in the lawful Jewish method. Those who do not ascribe themselves to the Jewish religion must be offered up as sacrifices to the High God."

The question arises, what will happen to the convert to Judaism in the coming Age of *Tikkun Olam*, the so-called Golden Age and New World Order? The converts will not be hated and treated murderously, as will be the Christians and other goyim. According to Dr. Israel Shahak, in his exceptional volume, *Jewish History, Jewish Religion*, these few souls are, in reality, not Gentile at all:

> "Those who convert to Judaism are, in reality 'Jewish souls' who got lost when Satan sexually violated the Holy Lady (*Shekinah* or *Matronit*, one of the female components of the one Godhead, sister and wife of the younger male God according to the Cabala) in her heavenly abode."

So, an exception is made for the convert, who is promised to be treated equally as are blood Jews but rarely is.

The dead are also hated by the Jews, so don't count on the grave as a hedge of protection against the vile Jews. Shahak writes, for example, that:

> "Jewish children are taught passages (in the Talmud) which command every Jew whenever passing near a cemetery to utter a blessing if the cemetery is Jewish, but to curse the mothers of the dead if it is non-Jewish."

"The Best of the Gentiles—Kill!"

The clearest indication of the hatred by Jews toward Gentiles is the Talmudic commandment, *"The best of the Gentiles—kill!"* Naturally, this law can only be exercised in a territory or region when the Jews have full authority. In wartime, this law is often imposed, and that is why so many Palestinians and Arabs are unmercifully treated and innocents captured and murdered.

A booklet published by the Central Regional Command of today's modern Israeli Army, written by the Chief Chaplain, gives this advice to soldiers:

> "When our forces come across civilians during a war or in hot pursuit or in a raid, so long as there is no certainty that those civilians are incapable of harming our forces, then according to Halakhah (the law) they may and even should be killed...

> "Under no circumstances should an Arab be trusted, even if he makes an impression of being civilized...

"In war, when our forces storm the enemy, they are allowed and even enjoined by the Halakhah to kill even good civilians, that is, civilians who are ostensibly good."

The commandment to kill without compunction in wartime applies equally to the elderly, the young, and to women. Thus, in an attack on Gaza in Palestine, it is not extraordinary to tally some 2,000 Palestinians slaughtered, compared to only 3 or 4 random Israeli deaths.

Murder of POWs Is Commonplace

The cruelty and conscienceless evil of the Jews is shown by the lethal nature of the Israeli Army in its 1973 war with neighboring Egypt. In 1998 an Israeli retired General exposed that Israel had, in the 1973 war, captured many thousands of Egyptian troops. Unwilling to comply with the Geneva Convention Laws of War, the Egyptians, defenseless with their hands tied behind their backs, were herded into the desert. There, they were all mercilessly slaughtered with machine guns. Then, bulldozers were used to crush them all into a huge bloody pit. This ungodly horror was kept from the world's media and conveniently covered up both by Israel and by the U.S. government.

Yitzak Rabin, the Israeli Commander who perpetrated this vicious act, had by 1998, been rewarded for his inhumane cruelty by being elected Prime Minister of Israel. Confronted with the evidence of this crime, Rabin arrogantly dismissed it as true, but so what? *"This is ancient history,"* he shrugged.

Of course, the supposed crimes of the Nazis against the Jews some three decades prior, were still being exposed and perpetrators prosecuted. They still are today, almost 20 years into the 21st century.

President Truman: Jews Guilty of Cruelty and Mistreatment

President Harry Truman, in July 1947, hit the nail on the head when he wrote of the Jews and their hatred and cruelty in his diary. Truman maintained that the Jews exceeded both Stalin and Hitler in their ferocity and hatred toward others outside their race:

"The Jews, I find, are very selfish. They care not how many Estonians, Latvians, Finns, Poles, Yugoslavs, or Greeks get murdered or mistreated... as long as the Jews get special treatment. Yet, when they have power, physical, financial, or political, neither Hitler nor Stalin has anything on them for cruelty and mistreatment to the underdog."

These comments in Truman's diary were unknown to the world until, finally, they were released on July 3, 2003 by the Truman Presidential Museum and Library. Evidently the "fear of Jews" had kept the cogent remarks bottled up for over half a century.

Killers of the Messiah and Their Own Prophets

It is the killing of their own prophets, Isaiah and others, and the killing of Jesus their Messiah, which best illustrates the burning hatred of the Jews. The Jews *need* a foreign culture to adequately exercise the demonic energies they so obviously possess. But if not, they will quickly eat their own kind. Thus, the Apostle Paul, himself a Jew, in *I Thessalonians 2:15* wrote of the Jews:

President Harry Truman, shown here in his Masonic regalia, said of the Jews, "...neither Hitler nor Stalin has anything on them for cruelty and mistreatment to the underdog."

> *"Who both killed the Lord Jesus and their own prophets, and have persecuted us, and they please not God, and are contrary to all men."*

It is no accident that Israel Shamir, an Israeli citizen who fought for Israel in the Yom Kippur War of 1973, sadly admits that the Jews are infected with the *"evil idea of Jewish supremacy."* Shamir, a decent man fed up with the many bigots in his country, calls Israel *"a Ku Klux Klan state run by madmen"* (Speech, Emory University, 2001).

FOURTEEN

Freemasonry and Judaism Worship the Same Egyptian Gods

"Ye are of your father the devil, and the lusts of your
father ye will do. He was a murderer from the beginning,
and abode not in the truth, because there is no truth in him.
When he speaketh a lie, he speaketh of his own: for he is a
liar, and the father of it."
                                   —*John 8:44*

"Yes, the (Egyptian god) Osiris does live in the darkness
and shadows of the Masonic lodges and temples...He was
the God of Solomon and is the reason God tore the
Kingdom of Israel from Solomon's throne. Solomon died
serving the God of Egypt."
                                   — Reginald Haupt, Jr.
                                   The Gods of the Lodge

In studying the sacred books of the Jews, the Talmud and the
Kabbalah, and also those of Freemasonry for more than a
quarter of a century, there is one conclusion I have come
to—that the God of the Jews and the God of the Masons is the same God.

139

And his name is Satan.

Of course, both the potentates of the Masonic Lodge and the chief rabbis of Judaism will say this is not so. Their own holy books instruct these demonic rulers to lie and conceal. But what I say here is so, and in my newest, heavily documented work, *Conspiracy of the Six-Pointed Star*, I prove it.

The Gods of the Lodge

Another book we are offering through the ministry also proves that Satan is "God" of both the Masonic Lodge and the Synagogue. This book, *The Gods of the Lodge*, by Reginald C. Haupt, Jr., deals a harsh and real blow to the ambitious, but wicked, aims of Freemasonry. I was privileged to write a foreword for this outstanding book and in it, I make mention of Haupt's astute observation that Freemasonry is not only *a* religion, but is, in fact, *the* basis for all pagan religions, including Talmudic Judaism. Masonry is nothing less than the ancient Egyptian Religion, decorated with arcane symbols and signs and painted with deceptive and worthless Judaic terminology.

What is most interesting is that each of these two sides of the same old and tired Egyptian religion—Masonry and Judaism—end up assuring the hopeful, but deceived, candidate that by proceeding through a bunch of silly rituals and by *rejecting* the firm foundation of Jesus Christ and His doctrines, the candidate can attain his own godhood. Yes, the dumbed-down Mason or Jew really comes to believe that he can become a deity, even a "Christ."

The Builders of the New World Order

What supreme trickery to build up a person's pride so excessively that he fancies himself *"perfected"* and deserving of a noble reign as King of a Kingdom. The Masons boast that their leaders are "Master Builders." So, too, do the rabbis claim they are building a kingdom. Satan, no doubt, enjoys this little bit of deceit, and he is preparing to take advantage of this grotesque theater of the absurd by producing an antichrist to ascend the throne of this Judeo-Masonic Kingdom once it is born on planet earth. Satan's minions have even spruced up their presentation and have adopted a new name for this kingdom—they call it the *New World Order*.

In *The Gods of the Lodge*, Haupt quotes one Masonic authority after another who makes reference to their Egyptian-based religion and the god whom they wish to exalt as the Great Architect of the New World Order. The chief deity is Osiris, and the Mason's encyclopedia teaches that:

"The promise of life is Osiris. The great doctrine, the great revelation of all the true Mysteries, is that Osiris lives: but he is known by other names. We also, as Masons, look forward to union...with Osiris...To be united with him forever."

The Egyptian trinity, Osiris and Isis and their son, Horus. Note the serpents atop the head of the Queen and the Son.

In "attaining perfection," the same Mason's encyclopedia assures the Masonic candidate that he *"becomes an Osiris, or incarnation of Deity."*

In other words, the Mason imagines that his pagan anti-Christian religion, based on the ancient Mysteries of Egypt, will actually confer Deity (godhood) on him. Is this not part of the Strong Delusion prophesied in *II Thessalonians 2?*

Man-made Traditions Spawned by Satan

W. L. Wilmshurst, 33°, recognized as one of the foremost authorities in the Masonic Lodge, emphasizes that the Hebrew traditions are based on the Egyptianism that preceded the Jews' religion. And, in fact, the Scriptures record Jesus Christ as telling the Jews that their religion, which they insisted was of Abraham and Moses, was (and is today) in fact of *"man-made traditions."* Christ bluntly informed the Jews that they were thus *not* of Abraham but, instead, are Satan's children:

"Ye are of your father the devil, and the lusts of your father ye will do. He was a murderer from the beginning and abode not in the truth..." (John 8:44)

It is true that Satan possesses a certain type of divine wisdom—that of the Serpent. Indeed, he is referred to in the book of Revelation as "that old serpent," and so the Jews' religion is that of the Serpent, for Jesus stated forthrightly that the Devil is the *"father"* of the Jews.

Head and Body of the Serpent

Kabbalistic rabbis do not mince words in confessing that the Serpent is their Lord and Savior. As I demonstrate in *Conspiracy of the Six-Pointed Star*, the Jewish teachers say that he, the Serpent, is their Head, and they, the Jewish nation, are the Body of the Serpent. This is why, in the Talmud, the sacred law book of Judaism, we find the provision that on the Sabbath, one *"is permitted to charm snakes and serpents."* Serpents, some Jewish rabbis claim, can thus be commanded to go and do a Jew's bidding—for example, striking an enemy.

Likewise, in Masonry, at the higher levels it is taught that the *"Holy Serpent"* represents the Masonic trinity of deities. He is the God of Forces. This knowledge of Serpent pre-eminence, writes Rex Hutchens, 33°, in his Masonic textbook, *A Bridge to Light*, is essential for the 32nd and 33rd degree candidates.

Hiram the Masonic Christ and Leviathan, the Jewish Messiah

The Masons and the Jews assert that assisting the Serpent in this common Mystery Religion will be a unique, all-wise, crafty leader. The Masons, in their literature and rituals, call this leader "Hiram Abiff," and he is a Christ figure. Wilmshurst, in his authoritative Masonic textbook, *The Meaning of Masonry*, writes:

> "Now the Hebrew word for Hiram means 'Guru,' teacher of 'Supreme Knowledge,' divine light and wisdom."

As Haupt explains and clarifies in *The Gods of the Lodge*, "Hiram" is given credit in the Lodge as being the "Master Architect." It is taught in Masonry that the much-revered Hiram "was assassinated, buried, and rose again." So here we have, in the Masonic Lodge, a satanic counterfeit of Christ Jesus.

Meanwhile, in Judaism, the rabbis change the names while preaching the same identical doctrines from hell. In the Jewish myth, the "Christ" is represented to be the Serpent whose name is "Leviathan." Now this

Egyptian gods and goddesses with their serpent coverings and protectors.

Serpent, the rabbis lament, was in past history banished to the dark, lower regions, the abyss, of the Tree of Life. But, they exult, Leviathan shall rise. Resurrecting, he will regain his liberty and emerge on the world scene to punish the "enemies" of the Jews (i.e. the Christians and Moslems).

Leviathan, the Serpent Deity, will establish a Kingdom of the Jews on planet earth. And, the Talmud adds, all Gentiles must then serve the Jews as their slaves. Either that or they shall be beheaded.

Osiris and The Rebuilding of the Temple of Solomon

In the Lodge, Hiram, it turns out, is the "Widow's Son" and moreover, is the earthly image of Osiris. He will rebuild the Temple of Solomon in

Jerusalem when he returns in glory. Likewise, the Jews say they will be led by a new "King David," their name for "Hiram," who, possessed by the divine wisdom of the Serpent, will—you got it—rebuild the Temple of Solomon.

Hiram, say the Masons, will hold the honored title of "Osiris," and not only that, but all who are perfected and made divine will be accorded this title. Wilmshurst explains:

> "In the great Mystery System of Egypt, which long anteceded the Hebrew system, the regenerate candidate, who has achieved the highest measure of self-transmutation of his lower nature, was accorded the title of Osiris. It was the equivalent of attaining Christhood."

As was Osiris, the once mere man is transformed into Deity:

> "Just as the limbs of the risen Osiris were said to reunite into a new whole…from the tomb and…transmuted into one of supernatural substance and splendor."

Worship of the Star God

You will recall that God commanded the Hebrew people to "come out of Egypt," but as the Christian martyr Stephen revealed in *Acts 6* and *7*, while sojourning in the desert for forty years, the Hebrews backslid into worship of the ancient Egyptian gods. Indeed, Stephen rightly accused them of setting up and worshipping the "Star," symbol of an Egyptian deity.

This star is today the Jews' six-pointed star and is found not only on the national flag of Israel but in almost every Jewish community, especially at Synagogues.

Not surprisingly, this same symbol of demonic Egypt is also prominently displayed in and on Masonic temples and lodges throughout the world. In fact, the most well known Masonic symbol, the square and compass, is nothing more than a stylized six-pointed star.

Egyptian Statues and Architecture

Their six-pointed star icon and idol is yet another proof that Freemasonry

Egyptian King Tut and Queen Nefertiti with their cobra headdresses. The Egyptian gods and goddesses bear great resemblance to the deities of the Jewish Kabbalah.

and Judaism are twin sisters in religious evil and in promoting Egyptianism. But there is more. The Masons often openly display Egyptian-themed statues and architecture. Meanwhile, in modern-day Israel we discover that the buildings housing the Supreme Court of Israel are of Egyptian-Masonic design, complete with obelisks. An Egyptian obelisk has been erected on the grounds of Hebrew University, and an Egyptian pyramid monument graces the boulevard of the Israeli city of Eilat. The wealthy Rothschild family has funded much of this occultic Egyptian architecture.

Moreover, what we find today, most regrettably, is that the so-called "Christian World" is also permeated with Egyptian and Satanic doctrines and symbology. Southern Baptist, Methodist, Episcopal and other churches are packed with members who are Freemasons. Their ranks include many pastors. Most of these churches, especially the Baptists, are also radically pro-Zionist. In evangelical churches, rabbinical Judaism is revered and promoted, and entire congregations are led to believe that the Judaic religion is holy and good, and that it is based solely on the Old Testament. The people in the pews have no idea that both the Masonic Lodge and the Jewish synagogues are snake pits of Egyptian religion.

God's Word is Truth

If only these people would cast aside the lies and myths taught them by their deceived pastors and leaders and, instead, read the Scriptures for themselves, the amazing truth would shine forth with clarity and power.

They would know and understand, for example, that God's Word identifies Jerusalem and Israel as the last days *"Sodom and Egypt" (Revelation 11)*. And they would be alert to the fact that it is the *"Synagogue of Satan" (Revelation 2 and 3)* that is Satan's primary tool today for destruction and enslavement of souls. It is also the root cause of so many prophetic horrors to come.

Let us pray, then that many of these otherwise good people will, indeed, open their Holy Bible and read its vital, life-saving passages. As Jesus our Lord emphasized, *"Ye shall know the truth, and the truth shall make you free" (John 8:32)*.

FIFTEEN

The Jewish Religion Teaches That Jews Are A Divine Species

"We Shall Be Our Own Messiah"

"And the serpent said...Ye shall not surely die...Ye shall
be as gods; knowing good and evil."
> — *Genesis 3*

"The Jewish people as a whole will became its own
Messiah... Thus will the promise of the Talmud be
fulfilled..."
> — Baruch Levy,
> Letter to Karl Marx, reprinted
> in *La Revue de Paris*, p. 574
> June 1, 1928

I visited a so-called "Christian" bookstore recently for the first time in years. But Christian it was not! Everywhere were signs of Judaism and of a poisonous form of Judeo-Christianity.

I was especially interested in the many books warning of the antichrist to come—the evil man with the prophetic identification number 666. It seems in vogue to claim that this man will be a Moslem. The books say that he will lead the Moslem hordes in killing Christians throughout the world. He shall be the Islamic antichrist. Allah is his "God," and Mohammed is his prophet.

Now the Jews must get a real kick out of seeing gullible "Christians" so easily deceived. These silly notions of an Arab antichrist are, in fact, being promoted these days by Jewish rabbis who, privately, laugh and hee-haw.

In my encyclopedic book, *Conspiracy of the Six-Pointed Star*, I reveal the biblical truths of the antichrist. Read my book—or obtain my CD or audiotape on this subject—and know.

Let me let you in on a big, big OPEN secret. It is a secret published widely by our Lord Jesus Christ who clearly is not impressed over the Arab future to come. This secret involves yet another group we are to watch, a terrible, inhuman, cruel sect He calls the *"Synagogue of Satan"* *(Revelation 2:9 and 3:9).*

The Jews and Their Messiah

Now the Jews would not be caught dead (excuse the pun) in an Islamic mosque. But the synagogue? Oh, yeah, that's their exclusive bailiwick. Their Messiah—not Jesus, but the Jews' Messiah—will reign and teach in the synagogue. The book of Revelation tells us about this abominable place of worship. The Jewish Messiah, according to the top rabbis, will not be an independent, external deity. He will merely represent them as king. Instead, the Jews are *The Chosen*—they are confident they shall be their own Messiah.

This I discovered in investigating the New Age movement, which is, in fact, a satanic movement authored by the Jews. When the Jews speak of "God," they refer to themselves.

Oh sure, Messiah shall come, they teach. He will be the new "Moses," the Davidic seed. But like Moses, like King David, he will not be God, but will, rather *serve God*. And who is God but the Jews themselves. The Jewish Messiah/king will be like all the Jews. They are collectively divine beings, gods on earth. He will be one of them: a god among gods.

The Jews as Collective Messiah—A Collection of Jewish Divine "Sparks"

Rabbi Yitzchak Ginsburgh, author of *What You Need to Know About the*

Kabbalah, points to the doctrine of Ba'al Shem Tav, the most famous rabbinical authority, who taught of the "immanent omnipresence of the almighty, which implies a unique equivalence between God and Creation." Ginsburgh says this equivalence means that, "God is all and all is God."

According to Ginsburgh, the Shekinah Presence, a divine spark or energy force, is found only in spiritually advanced Jews. God is an "aggregate," or combination of these sparks, and the Messiah is made up of the divine sparks, the sanctified elite. These divine beings collectively shall usher in the Messianic Age.

Rabbi David Cooper explains further that the "coming of Messiah" is actually the "coming of messianic consciousness." Men who become divine *realize* their divinity and become fully *conscious*.

Planet of God—Paradise on Earth?

The *"Planet of God,"* a concept of Robert Mueller, former administrative head at the United Nations, is achieved when this Messianic Age is created. An elite of super-souls, conscious god-men, shall rule and reign. There is no single "God." As Nietzsche informed us, the "Super Men" shall rule. Billy Phillips, teacher at *kabbalahstudent.com*, says that in the *Zohar*, a book of the Kabbalah, we discover:

"Kabbalah explains that when the new reality arrives our planet
will change its physical dimension, enlarging... The borders of the
land of Israel will extend and include the entire planet and all
people.

"However, the Messiah arrives only when individual people
achieve a personal state of Messiah within themselves. Once a
critical mass and specific threshold of people achieve this
personal, individual state, only then will the global Messiah appear
as a seal and not a savior.

"The Messiah is a seal that confirms that we, the people, have
achieved true transformation of our own nature, and turn the
planet.

"After this state of Messiah is achieved, there will be one thousand years of paradise on earth, according to Kabbalah… That is the true Super Earth."

Serve the Jews, or Be Beheaded

Ah yes, a super Earth, with super "Masters," will mean paradise, or Utopia, for all mankind. Well, not all mankind, but all who worship and serve their Jewish overlords. Others will be summarily executed, beheaded, says the Talmud.

So, the Jews point to a "God," but theirs is a collective "God"—the Jews of the world. They alone are the divine god-men recognized by the Kabbalah and Talmud. The Gentiles, an inferior species, will be grouped under the Jews and will serve them. Those who refuse or are not fit shall be killed. That is the talmudic law.

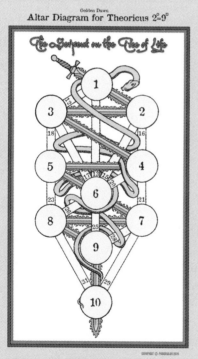

The Holy Serpent ascending on the Jewish Tree of Life, complete with all his gods and goddesses.

The Holy Serpent—an artist's depiction of the serpent and the Tree of Life.

"The Messianic Age will be marked by the triumph of Jewish exclusiveness, in which the reign of justice means the strict observance of the Law of Yahweh...in a word, Jewish law... The nations will be converted to Judaism and obey the law or else they will be destroyed and the Jews will be masters of the world." (*La Vérite Israelite*, vol. V, p.74, France)

The Serpent Shall Ascend to the Crown

The Jews, then, will be their own Messiah. The Kabbalah tells us that Jews shall rise from the depths of the abyss. First, the goddess Malkuth, united sexually with her phallic consort, Hesod, shall elevate them upwards, toward the Crown of Life. Along the way, the Serpent shall watch over and guide the Jews. The Serpent is their symbol, providing chaos and destruction of the world of the Gentiles. From this chaos and destruction comes, finally, order. *Order out of Chaos.*

This is why the Jews, including today's top rabbis and leaders like Netanyahu, have convinced themselves of the usefulness of nuclear bombs. Before Israel falls as a nation, she intends to resort to the "Samson Option"— The Jews will unleash their nuclear bombs on targets. Those targeted include the Arabs, European and Russian capitals, and the United States

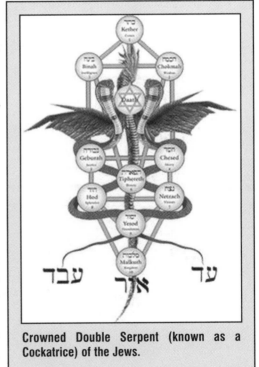

Crowned Double Serpent (known as a Cockatrice) of the Jews.

of America. Out of the ashes shall come the rising, magnificent *Phoenix* bird, Israel.

Michael Collins Piper addresses this important topic in his excellent book, *The Golem—Israel's Nuclear Hell Bomb and the Road to Global Armageddon.*

The Jews Are Demonically Insane

Let's face it. Any people, or race, or nation, that looks in the mirror and stupidly proclaims, *"I am Chosen...I am God...I am my Own Messiah... All others are mere beasts"* is, by definition, insane. God promised He would drive such arrogant men insane, and He has done so.

And all who support this narcissistic garbage have, themselves, become wildly insane. They have, in fact, fallen into a profoundly, intoxicating Mystery of Iniquity, a terrible revolt against God and His true Kingdom. Christian Zionist, that means you!

SIXTEEN

Jews Claim Their Blood is Divine. Their Racism has had Terrible Consequences

Are Jews the Master Race?

"The Jews are human beings, but the Goyim (Gentiles) are only beasts."

— *Babylonian Talmud (114a-b)*

As a young man, I read many stories about the German Nazis. Supposedly, the Nazis believed that Aryans were the "Master Race." This Master Race ideology was said to have propelled the Nazis to do horrible things to some other races, whom they deemed to be inferior.

Later, as an adult, I discovered that the Soviet Union and the West had also perpetrated terrible acts against the Germans, including the heinous fire-bombing of Dresden and the massacre of helpless German POWs and of millions of innocent German civilians. The Allies, under the directions of the Jews, history reveals, were responsible for the mass roundup and murder of innocent German civilians—men, women, and children—who were herded *after the war* into concentration camps.

I also read about some prejudiced Whites who once thought that they, too, were a superior race, far above the Blacks. This ideology enabled them to pass laws to keep the Blacks subordinate, and for years even made them into slaves.

But while Blacks were treated abusively as slaves, it is also true that, as history's archives show, it was mainly Jewish slave traders who abducted, shipped, and sold the slaves around the world and especially in the U.S.A.

Today, the world continues to suffer under the false idea of a "Master Race." Now it is the Jews who are claiming that they are superior to all other "inferior" races. The Jews own holy book, the Talmud (formally called the *Babylonian Talmud*), as well as their Kabbalah, declare the Jews to be destined to conquer and subjugate the "non-Jews," and to kill all who oppose this quest. The Talmud states: *"The best of the Gentiles— Kill."*

We alone are God's Chosen, say the rabbis, no matter how wicked we are.

Now, logic tells us that while inequality is a fact of life—we *are* all unequal in one way or another, in good looks, strength, intelligence, talent, ability, etc.—we should not treat our fellowman as either inferior or superior. Especially due solely to their race or color.

To consider any one race or set of people as a "Master Race" and superior is especially notorious and harmful to society. Judging a man primarily by the content of his character and not on his color seems to me prudent and wise.

God No Respecter of Persons

The Holy Bible affirms that God is no respecter of persons. *"Whosoever will"* may come, that is His great and magnificent rule *(Romans 2:11)*. Each of us, of whatever race, ethnic group, nation, color or DNA makeup, who has faith in Jesus Christ as Lord will be saved. There is no flesh in heaven, Jew, Gentile or otherwise. The Bible says that our human flesh eventually returns to the dust of the earth. A saved person thankfully is born again, "in spirit and in truth" *(John 3:3)*.

As for our belonging to a certain race, *Galatians 3:29* is clear. It says that Gentile, Jew, it doesn't mean a thing. Every person who has Christ Jesus is *"Abraham's seed and heirs according to the promise."*

Jews Exhibit a Poisonous Racial Attitude

It was only about 20 years ago when I first discovered that the Jews today continue to exhibit a poisonous racial attitude toward others. The Apostle Paul reported two millennia ago on this unseemly Jewish doctrine, writing of the Jews:

"Who both killed the Lord Jesus, and their own prophets, and have persecuted us; and they please not God, and are contrary to all men" (I Thes. 2:15)

According to their own most holy book, *The Babylonian Talmud*, which virtually every rabbi and observant Jew holds to be true, the Jew is superior and is a totally different species than others:

"The Jews are human beings, but the goyim (Gentiles) are not human beings; they are only beasts" *(Baba Mezia 114a-114b).*

Inferior Gentiles, says the Talmud, are destined to be the Jews' slaves:

"The non-Jew is an animal in human form, and is condemned to serve the Jew day and night" *(Midrash Talpiah 225).*

Jews Claim to Be a Divine Species

Wondering if it was only the most bigoted and hateful of the Jews who would believe such passages, I then set out to research their own writings. What I found shocked me. Over and over, in their speeches and books, Jewish authorities make clear that Jews are a special people, superior to Gentiles, a divine species, even "gods" on earth.

Here are a few selected quotes. I'll be glad to provide hundreds of other quotes. There can be no doubt. Modern Jews are possessed by an all-consuming spirit of bigotry and a haughty arrogance never seen before in human hearts. Only a devil could dream these up.

"Since the Jews are the highest and most cultured people on earth, the Jews have a right to subordinate the rest of mankind and to be the masters of the earth."
—Rabbi Harry Waton

"The Jewish people as a whole will become its own Messiah. It will attain world domination by the dissolution of other Races… Thus will the promise of the Talmud be fulfilled."
—Baruch Levy, letter to Karl Marx

"All non-Jews are evil by nature. The Jews are the crown of creation, the non-Jews are the scum of the earth.
—Rabbi Shneur Zalman

"We have to recognize that Jewish blood and the blood of a goy (Gentile) are not the same thing. Every law that is based on equating goys and Jews is completely unacceptable."
—Rabbi Yitzchak Ginsburgh

"The blood of the Jewish people is loved by the Lord; it is therefore redder and their life is preferable."
—Rabbi Yitzhak Ginsburgh

"One million Arabs are not worth a Jewish fingernail."
—Rabbi Yaacov Perrin

"We have a case of the Jew...a totally different species. The body of a Jewish person is of a totally different quality from the body of members of other nations of the world... A non-Jewish person comes from three satanic spheres, while the Jewish world stems from holiness."
—Rabbi Mendel Schneerson

"Everything about us is different. Jews are ontologically (biologically) exceptional."
—Elie Wiesel, holocaust activist

"Jewish blood is not the same as the blood of a Gentile."
—Rabbi Yitzhak Ginsburgh

"According to the Talmud, one may kill any Gentile."
—Rabbi Ido Elba

"A Jew who kills a non-Jew is exempt from judgement and has not violated the prohibition of murder."
—Rabbi Israel Ariel

Please understand that these quotes are not from rabbis who lived centuries ago. Most of these men are alive today and are quoted often by the Jewish press. The Talmud itself is said by famous Jewish writer Herman Wouk *(Winds of War)* to be the *"Jews' life blood."* U.S. Supreme Court Justice Ruth Bader Ginsburg calls the Talmud, *"My sacred, daily guide for living."*

All these famous rabbis and other Jews are following strictly the rules and laws of their Talmud which actually tells the Jews that, someday, when the Jews receive their kingdom, *"Even the best of the Gentiles will be put to death."* Beheading is the method of execution, says the Talmud.

DNA Science Proves Jews Are Not Special

My latest book, ***DNA Science and the Jewish Bloodline***, is especially despised by the rabbis precisely because, in this book, I report modern DNA research which finds that the modern "Jews" are not descendants of Abraham. They are not even Israelite, or of Jewish blood. Their DNA shows that almost every Jew alive on earth today descended from the Khazarians, a people of Turkish and Mongol origins.

So the rabbinical malarkey about the Jews being "special" and of a "different species" is absolutely wrong.

Why Do Pastors and Evangelists Hide This Knowledge?

Why is it that no pastor in America professes to know what the Talmud says about the Jews being the "Master Race?" Why is it that Pastor Joel Osteen, Pastor Rick Warren, Franklin Graham, John Hagee, Kenneth Copeland—no, not even the Catholic Pope Francis nor any one of some 200 Catholic Cardinals—has the courage and the guts to inform you and me of this hideous crime, this tremendously evil and warped doctrine of the Jews.

I have heard plenty all my life about the evil Nazis. I am constantly told of the hatred some Whites once had toward Blacks. My eyes see evidence that many blacks today hate whites. But of the Jews arrogant race doctrine, nary a word. It's part of their Judaic religion. Why is this obvious fact covered up, never mentioned? Who gave the Jews the power to punish any who dare publish the facts of such obvious bigotry?

Why has no one, no one in the press, ever once asked or demanded that Justice Ruth Bader Ginsburg, or Judge Breyer, or Judge Sotomayor—all Jews on the Supreme Court—renounce the hatred and bigotry of the Talmud?

There are 535 U.S. Senators and Congressmen. Why have *none* of those U.S. politicians, nor one of 50 state governors, warned us of this evil race doctrine of the Jews?

Terrible Consequences

Ideas have consequences, and the Jews' satanic idea that their "blood" and "flesh" is different and is superior has lead to some very terrible consequences. Just ask historians about the 66 million Russian citizens slain by the Jews in the Soviet Union, or ask about the many thousands of Palestinians murdered, raped, and plundered since 1948 by Israel.

For me, I do not hesitate to say with Christian determination in my heart, that the Nazis who held the Aryan race doctrine were wrong. The White slavers and today's whites who hate blacks were likewise wrong. And today's Black racists are wrong.

To these groups I add the Jew. Not all Jews and, of course, history tells us that not all Nazis nor all Whites and Blacks were, or are, bigots. But today's Jews deserve a special place in hell because this racial nonsense remains their official religious doctrine. It is reiterated over and over in their holy book, the Babylonian Talmud. And it has been there as a consuming seed of poisonous, boiling hatred for more than 2,000 years.

"American Jews are actually trained since childbirth to interact with non-Jews in a deceitful and arrogant manner," admits Karen Friedman, herself a Jew, in her Internet blog. "They actually coordinate with each other to emotionally destroy non-Jews and Israel critics." This, she adds, "is actually deliberate, wicked, planned behavior motivated by a narcissistic, self-righteous fury."

"The Jew doesn't care how much he or she hurts others," warns Ms. Friedman. "Jews only care about what's good for the Jews."

The Jews: Unequalled in Race Hatred and Bigotry

No one can match the Jews in their passionate race hatred and bigotry. The days of slavery are long past. The time of the Nazi is far-gone. But evil Judaism lives on. Satan survives and prospers in the hearts of the Jews. Jesus prophesied this bigotry. He said that the Jews are led by Satan and that, consequently, the house of Israel is *"left desolate" (Matthew 23:38).*

If you are fearful of the Jews and so, keep quiet, you, too, are jointly guilty of the sin of bigotry and hate. By your silence, you become an accomplice to these devilish rabbis and their kin. May our God in heaven, who loves and holds equally worthy and accountable every man who believes in Him and serves Him in faith, strengthen you in spirit and give you boldness to stand up to the Jews and tell the truth.

SEVENTEEN

Jewish Homosexuals Fought Against Romans in Rebellion, 66-70 AD

Ancient Homosexual Warriors Make Comeback in Israel

"Just got back from an all expenses paid trip to Tel Aviv—gay capital of the world, Wow! So many hot dudes. Who cares if they have turned the Gaza Strip into one big concentration camp when it's PARTY time here."
                                        —*Fagburn*, February 4, 2013

American evangelicals, who revere Israel as the "Holy Land" and as the home of God's Chosen, may want to reconsider their diseased theology. In fact, Israel is home to some of the world's most energetic and active gays and lesbians—men and women who not only have same sex but regularly mock and despise our Lord Jesus Christ.

The Apostle Paul, who warned against sexual uncleanness, lewdness, and fornication, would be appalled if he were to return to Israel today. Paul specifically names "homosexuals" and "sodomites" as among those who will *not* inherit the kingdom of God *(I Corinthians 6:9-10)*.

Government of Israel Foots the Bill

The perverse Israeli government of Benjamin Netanyahu continues to spend millions of U. S. taxpayer dollars promoting a filthy and open display of sexual carnality by Israel's gays. For example, the government officially endorsed the annual Gay Pride World Festival held each July in Tel Aviv.

It was the Orwellian Ministry of Truth that paid the bills for thousands of American gays to travel to Israel this year to participate in the revelry. The publisher of *Fagburn*, a blog promoting gays and their culture, had his trip paid for by the Ministry of Truth.

Fagburn actually congratulated the Israeli government for its genocidal attacks on Palestine and for its "killing of children." They are clearing the beaches of Palestinians for "gay holiday resorts," blared *Fagburn* in a recent edition. "Fab!" said the gay website.

Fagburn went on to remark, "Who cares if they have turned the Gaza Strip into one big concentration camp when it's PARTY time here."

Palestinians have noticed that although many of their Israeli Defense Forces soldiers are cruel and vicious, the worst seem to be the homosexuals. "They will kill you in an instant, then laugh and spit on your dead corpse," lamented one Palestinian.

Amazingly, the cowardly Orthodox Jews refuse to serve in the Israeli military. They have been exempted from military service by the courts. This leaves the way open for gays and lesbians to enter. Many psychopathic "warriors" join the armed forces and brag that they now have a license to kill the Palestinians, whom they deem to be "inferior beasts." The Babylonian Talmud, their most holy book, confirms their brutal treatment of the Palestinian population.

Historian Josephus Reports on the Homosexual Jewish Warriors

That the gay warriors of Israel came from a long tradition is proven by the writings of the great Jewish historian, Josephus. Josephus, in reporting on the Jewish rebellion (66-70 AD) against the Romans, stated there were principally three Jewish factions fighting against the roman army of Titus and Vespesian, which had laid siege to Jerusalem.

These three factions hated and fought each other, and so, the Roman army laid back to see how much damage and chaos they would do to *each other* before advancing.

One of the factions was the Galilean gangs of John of Gischala, whose members were reprobate homosexuals. Their "degenerate practices" were distasteful to the Zealots and others who warred against them.

Josephus reported that this homosexual faction of warriors adopted peculiar methods:

> "Not content with looting throughout the city, they unscrupulously engaged in effeminate practices, plaiting their hair and attiring themselves in women's apparel, drenching themselves with perfumes and painting their eyelids to enhance their beauty... Yet, while they wore women's faces, their hands were murderous, and approaching with mincing steps they would suddenly become warriors and whipping out their swords from under their dyed mantles, transfix whomsoever they met."

With these perfumed and painted homosexual Jewish warriors decimating their opponents, the path of the Romans was made relatively easy. Michael Grant, in *The Jews in the Roman World*, wrote that, "The Jews were destroying themselves by their extraordinary disunity, quite as effectively as the whole Roman army could."

This result was exactly as was prophesied by Jesus in 33 AD. It was

Josephus, the famous Jewish historian, wrote of the victory of the Romans and the putrid role of the Jewish homosexuals in that conflict.

the victory of Roman General Titus who utterly destroyed the city of Jerusalem, unmercifully massacred the homosexual Jewish warriors, and left not one rock on top another of the Jewish Temple built by their Idumean King, Herod.

Jewish Gays Wreck American Culture

Today, in the United States, it has been the Jews who have led the people into a confused tar patch of wicked homosexuality. Jews are the founders of almost all the gay organizations. The Southern Poverty Law Center, an evil, propaganda-spewing Jewish group, is pro-gay all the way, and the son of Abraham Foxman, head of the ungodly group, the ADL, is the husband (or wife?) of a homosexual marriage partner.

Though Jews themselves rarely serve in the U.S. military, being duel citizens of Israel and for the most part, unpatriotic to America, they enthusiastically support gays and transgenders in our armed forces. The Babylonian Talmud, which the rabbis strongly endorse, is said to be a book devoted to radical sexual liberation. As Jonas Alexis, a noted Christian author and researcher stresses in his excellent book, *Christianity and Rabbinic Judaism*, "Following Talmudic mores, these people have abandoned moral restraints and are weakening the Biblical Christian foundation of America."

They'll Kill You and Think They Do God Service

Homosexuals, contrary to what the media report, are not innocent and friendly bystanders of American culture. They are "reprobates," the Bible reports. They hasten to murder. First the Jews, next the Romans, now, in the 21st century, the Christians. As Josephus warned, while they wear women's faces, their hands are murderous. They will kill you and think they do God service.

EIGHTEEN

Protocols of the Learned Elders of Zion—Path of the Serpent

"A prudent man foreseeth the evil, and hideth himself; but the simple pass on, and are punished."
—Proverbs 27:12

"Today, I may tell you that our goal is now only a few steps off. There remains a small space to cross and the whole long path we have trodden is ready now to close its cycle of the Symbolic Snake, by which we symbolize our people."
— The Protocols of the Learned Elders of Zion (Protocol No. 3)

C ommunist butcher Vladimir Lenin had them memorized by heart. A copy of them lay on his bedstand, and he read them with ferocious and apt attention. *"What brilliance!,"* Lenin must have thought. *"What fierce intelligence...what bold audacity the devil inspires in my dark heart through his Protocols of Zion!"*

By the time Hitler rose to become Chancellor of Germany, the Jewish Communists—Lenin, Trotsky, Kaganovich, Yagoda and others—had already carried out the most diabolical and gruesome holocaust and series of death purges ever perpetrated on a suffering humanity.

Russian people suffered during the communist era under the savagery of Jewish butchers and mad men.

Thousands of Gulag prison camps, mobile gas chambers, and blood-spattered police interrogation centers were in full operation throughout the Soviet Union. According to noted Russian researcher Aleksandr Solzhenitsyn (author of *The Gulag Archipelago*), some sixty-six million men, women, and children were arrested, imprisoned, bludgeoned, tortured, and executed. Still, Lenin kept howling at associates: *More... More blood... More terror. Do it! Now!*

For over fifty years I have made it my life's occupation to study the abomination that took place in Soviet Russia, followed by the lethal chaos and pain in Eastern Europe and Red China. The immensity of these brutal crimes cannot be overestimated. Any offenses committed by Hitler—and I do not paint over such offenses—were puny and minor compared to what took place in the Soviet Empire from 1917 to 1984.

How did these Communist spiritual predators and ancestors of Barack Obama, Lord Rothschild, George Soros, Nancy Pelosi, and today's Wall Street bankers do it? How were they able to grip scores of nations by the throat and yank out the jugular vein of tens of millions of innocent people? I am convinced it was because Lenin, Stalin and the others were well-grounded in the *Protocols of Zion*.

The Protocols Were Their "Bible"—Pure Babylon

This was their "Bible," their operating manual. Its prescriptions had emerged from centuries of meticulous research and experimentation. Its conclusions had been tested by the Rothschilds, the Warburgs, by Marx and Hegel. Never had a manual of discourse so perfectly meshed with the labyrinth rules and laws set forth in the rabbis' Talmud. The Protocols were *Pure Babylon*, authored by human devils inspired by Beelzebub, Azazel, and all the other demons from the bottomless pit of the Jews abyss of Abaddon.

Seeing as I did the vast significance of the *Protocols of Zion*, I knew I must make them available to as large an audience as possible. Let me be clear. The Protocols of Zion is the most banned book in the world. The tyrants and killers do not want you to read this incredible volume. They are the book burners, the censors, the would-be despots of humanity who intend to herd you, me, and all of humanity into the cattle pen of slavery and humiliation. The Protocols is their blueprint, their roadmap.

The Protocols have been outlawed in nation after nation so that today, it is extremely difficult to obtain a copy. But necessity of survival and freedom of speech dictate that this book be made available to all who seek truth. That is why I have chosen to publish this latest edition, complete with my new Foreword.

The Serpent of the Protocols of Zion

The Holy Serpent figures prominently in the Protocols. According to the highest-ranking kabbalistic rabbis, the Serpent represents not only a specific deity, Lucifer, but also the whole nation, or people of Israel. The House of Israel, the collective of all the Jews wherever they may reside on this planet, is said to be the body of the Serpent. The head is claimed to be the Illuminati initiates who, behind the scenes, are masterminding and guiding the Serpent in his path of global dominion.

It is not simply that the most fanatical and zealous high priests of Judaism worship the divine Serpent; in the teachings of the Kabbalah, the Jewish People are the "Serpent." As such, as explained in the *Encyclopedia Judaica*, the Jewish People, as a whole, are their own *"Messiah."* Every Jew is divine while all other people (the *Goyim*, or Gentiles) are less than human and are privileged to even be alive. Indeed, the *Goyim*, the Talmud emphasizes, are beasts fit only to be servants and slaves of Jewish *effendi* (masters).

On the Sabbath One Is Permitted to Charm Snakes

The Talmud, the sacred law book of Judaism, includes a provision that on the Sabbath, one *"is permitted to charm snakes and serpents" (Sanhedrin 101a, 101b).*

To "charm" means to invoke, to invite or welcome, an entity (serpent or spirit) to come under your command and do your bidding. In this way, the beguiled snake could be induced by the charmer to stealthily seek out and destroy an enemy. The Zionist Serpent of Death, it is claimed, symbolically strikes at one enemy after another until all the world is bitten and defeated. But the Serpent, in Judaic lore, legend and sectarian doctrine, is more than a servant of the Jews. He is the Spiritual Director of the Great Work of the Illuminati Jews, and from the beginning, he brought to this planet his alchemical powers of deceit and seduction.

The Encyclopedia of American Jewish History (by Stephen Norton and Eunice Pollack, pp. 182-184) tells us that in the Kabbalah philosophies, the Star of David, with its twin triangles (masculine and feminine) are merged together, that is, they are fused—to become an integrated whole and thus represent the same thing. This signifies completion of the path of the Zionist Serpent who uses darkness and death as well as an occult form of light, illumination and enlightenment, to accomplish his purposes. This further signifies that *The Great Work* (*aka* the historical cycles of the Hegelian dialectical process) has been accomplished, and a Golden Age of Glory is realized. This will be the New Age during which the god-men (initiated Jews) shall reign supreme.

Judaism the Mystery Religion

Ancient Mystery religions particularly worshipped the Serpent as divine, and Judaism borrowed from these ancient teachings during the Jews' long captivity and sojourn in Babylon during and after Jeremiah's time. The Babylonians, Egyptians and the North African Ophites were deep into this strange and bizarre cultism. Throughout Mexico, Central and South America, the indigenous peoples worshipped the Serpent by such names as Quetzalcoatl and Kukulkan.

In many of these ancient religions and cultures, the high priests visualized the Serpent-God to be in the form of a circle, with the end of the serpent's tail inside the mouth of the beast. This was the *Oroboros*, a worm, snake, or dragon.

Symbolically, the Oroboros (also spelled *Ouroboros*, and *Auro Borus*) was said to represent both spiritual man and the earth passing, or evolving, through the cycles of reincarnation. Finally, at the final stage, in which the circular serpent grabs or consumes his own tail, he is regenerated as a perfected, divine creature.

The symbol of the Oroboros, the devouring serpent, is embraced by the kabbalist masters as a picture of the Jewish Nation or People. Empowered by supernatural force, the rabbis teach that the eternal Jewish People encircle and conquer the whole Earth, finally making all creatures and things subservient and passive. Next comes a transformation of the Earth—its mending and revision, or reconstruction (in Hebrew, *Tikkun Olam*), under the tutelage of a new, reincarnated King David who holds the crown (Kether) found atop the kabbalistic Tree of Life.

The Serpent's Role in Judaism

Thus, I was not surprised during my decades of studies into ancient and modern religions and cults to discover that the Holy Serpent plays a major—if not THE major—role in Judaism, the Pharisaic religion of the modern-day Jews. Among the most devoted of Jewish kabbalists (or cabalists), the Serpent is held to be a co-equal with God. Indeed, he is the flip side of Jehovah.

In recognition of this great God, the Serpent, the imperialistic ambitions of the Zionist Jews lead them to pay homage to their deity, whom, accordingly, they revere as the Symbolic Snake. In Protocol No. 3 of *The Protocols of the Learned Elders of Zion*, the Jewish co-conspirators are assured that total victory of Zionism and the exaltation of their esteemed leader, *"The Sovereign Lord of All the World,"* is very close:

"Today I may tell you that our goal is now only a few steps off. There remains a small space to cross and the whole long path we have trodden is ready now to close its cycle of the Symbolic Snake, by which we call our people."

The Global Trail of the Zionist Snake

Sergius Nilus, the first publisher of the Protocols in 1905, in studying this heinous blueprint of the Jews, discovered that there was a definite, chronological plan for the Zionist Snake to journey and conquer the nations until the whole world was vanquished and lay in its fatal embrace. He commented as follows:

> "According to the records of secret Jewish Zionism, Solomon and other Jewish learned men already, in 929 B.C., thought out a scheme in theory for a peaceful conquest of the whole universe by Zion.

> "As history developed, this scheme was worked out in detail and completed by men who were subsequently initiated in this question. These learned men decided by slyness of the Symbolic Snake, whose head was to represent those who have been initiated into the plans of the Jewish administration, and the body of the Snake to represent the Jewish people—the administration was always kept secret, even from the Jewish nation itself.

> "As this Snake penetrated into the hearts of the nations which it encountered, it undermined and devoured all the non-Jewish power of those States. It is foretold that the designed plan, until the course which it has to run is closed by the return of its head to Zion and until, by this means, the Snake has completed its round of Europe, and has encircled it—and until, by dint of enchaining

The symbol of the ouroboros, the devouring serpent, represents the Jewish people who encircle and conquer all other races. At the end of their successful journey, *Tikkun Olam* is achieved and the Jew becomes King and Ruler over all.

Europe, it has encompassed the whole world. This it is to accomplish by using every endeavour to subdue the other countries by an economical conquest.

"The return of the head of the Snake to Zion can only be accomplished after the power of all the Sovereigns of Europe has been laid low, that is to say, when by means of economic crises and wholesale destruction effected everywhere there shall have been brought about a spiritual demoralization and a moral corruption, chiefly with the assistance of Jewish women masquerading as French, Italians, etc. These are the surest spreaders of licentiousness into the lives of the leading men at the heads of nations.

"A map of the course of the Symbolic Snake is shown as follows: Its first stage in Europe in 429 B.C., in Greece, where, in the time of Pericles, the Snake first started eating into the power of that country. The second stage was in Rome in the time of Augustus, about 69 B.C. The third in Madrid in the time of Charles V., in 1552 A.D. The fourth in Paris about 1790, in the time of Louis XVI. The fifth in London from 1814 onwards (after the downfall of Napoleon). The sixth in Berlin in 1871 after the Franco-Prussian war. The seventh in St. Petersburg, over which is drawn the head of the Snake under the date of 1881.

"All these States which the Snake traversed have had the foundations of their constitutions shaken, Germany with its apparent power, forming no exception to the rule. In economic conditions England and Germany are spared, but only till the conquest of Russia is accomplished by the Snake, on which at present (i.e. 1905), all its efforts are concentrated. The further course of the Snake is not shown on this map, but arrows indicate its next movement towards Moscow, Kieff, and Odessa.

"It is now well known to us to what extent the latter cities form the centres of the militant Jewish race. Constantinople is shown as the last stage of the Snake's course before it reaches Jerusalem."

A World Program

This 1905 analysis by Sergius Nilus of the secret Zionist plan for the Symbolic Serpent (snake) to gradually and inexorably slither across the whole earth, constricting its victims in its coils and consuming huge expanses of territory until all of humanity is its victim and conquest, is astonishing for a number of reasons. We recall that famed industrialist Henry Ford in 1920 said that the Protocols of Zion were ingenious, if diabolical, and give us an exact and accurate picture of what actually has happened and is happening in world history.

Gold and Oil Treasures Are Aim of Zionist Serpent Forces

Next on the agenda of the Symbolic Snake of the coming Zionist King-Despot is the entire Middle East. Also in the eyes' view of the Serpent is the mineral-rich continent of Africa. The Zionists have aspirations to control the fabled gold and diamond mines of King Solomon. Egypt, Libya, the Sudan, Liberia, Rwanda, the Congo, South Africa and other African nations have so far been the focal point for Zionist action.

Having the industrialized and technology rich Western nations firmly in their lap, and with ancient enemy Iraq (Babylon) felled, and when two other ancient foes Iran (Persia) and Syria (Assyria) are conquered, the rich, black-gold stores of petroleum will be completely in the hands of the Zionist *Effendi* (masters). Combine that with the gold, silver, diamonds and other mineral treasures of Africa and you have total economic domination of Planet Earth.

Then we shall see the Gentiles go "off the rails"—vanquished and swallowed up by the all-consuming, slithering Serpent of Zion. Then shall be presented the One the Jews have groomed and prepared for planetary leadership—the one whom the *Protocols of Zion* gives the revealing title, *"The Sovereign Lord of All the World."*

In sum, the master plan of the Zionist elite who formulated their diabolical *Protocols of Zion*, entails the arcane Serpent of Death to traverse the globe, wrapping its ugly and horrifying body across the circular sphere of Earth. The adder's poisonous head, darkened like the ebony black of the dangerous African Mamba snake, is Rothschild, his inner circle, and the Jewish Sanhedrin. This viper's head will transform itself into the Son of Perdition, Satan's progeny, the Antichrist himself. Passing through the holy city of Bethlehem, this King-Despot of Zionism will establish his throne in Jerusalem. Then mankind shall see a brief spasm of ultimate evil such as the world has never known.

A Rough Beast Comes Forth

Thus we recall the amazingly prescient and prophetic words of the English poet, W.B. Yeats, who, in his eerily esoteric *The Second Coming* (1919), gave us a vision of the occult destiny to come when the enemies of Christ are someday on the very threshold of loosing their pitiless "blood-dimmed tide" upon the world.

> "Surely some revelation is at hand; Surely the Second Coming is at hand... And what rough beast, its hour come round at last, slouches toward Bethlehem to be born?"

Is This Not the Devil's Doing?

Please, read the Protocols and decide for yourself. Is this not the Devil's doing? More than that, ask yourself these momentous questions:

▲ Will the global conspirators use these same repugnantly wicked *Protocols of Zion* that so viciously devastated human hopes and brought such horrific tragedy in past decades to unleash the fury of an entirely new and even more bloody assault on human beings in this, our present-day era?

▲ Is America destined to replay and repeat this sad, torturous history as Satan's Zionist, Communist agents once again crank up their funeral engines of death and ignite with demonic passions their long pent-up, jack-booted Red Terror?

It is, indeed, wisely said that those who do not learn from history are doomed to repeat it. And so it is that the hoofbeats of the horsemen of the Apocalypse can already be heard not too far off in the distance. Prepare for their coming. Get ready. Study the profoundly revealing Holy Bible's book of Revelation; then carefully, very carefully, read and become forewarned of the Devil's stratagems and plan as revealed in the *Protocols of Zion*.

Always remember: It is the prudent man, steeped in the incomparable Word of God, but keenly aware of the Devil's crafty devices, who will remain safe and secure as mankind passes through the coming days of deception and despair.

NINETEEN

Sergius Nilus, Christian Saint and Prophet of God

The Man Who Gave the World the Protocols of Zion

"Best results in governing are attained by violence and terrorism. Freedom of the press, the right of association, freedom of conscience, the voting principle, and many others must disappear forever from the memory of men."
> — *Protocols of the Learned Elders of Zion*

"For more than half an hour I knelt...I told him about my sorrows, opened to him the whole of my sinful soul... everything lay like a heavy stone on my heart... For the first time, by the grace of God, I experienced with all my soul the experience of repentance...For the first time I felt that God, God Himself was sending me His forgiveness."
> — Sergius Nilus, quoted in *The New Martyrs and Confessors of Russia,* by Vladimir Moss

Amerika is gripped today by a threat far greater than any she has ever faced. It is the threat of *Zio-Mammonism,* a toxic blend of global imperialism which synthesizes the worst of cartel (monopolistic) capitalism with the most vicious form of communism.

The roots of Zio-Mammonism can be traced all the way back to decadent, pharisaic Jerusalem and Israel in the day of Jesus and His disciples. Jesus unmasked the Jews as a satanic sect filled with overbearing lust for money and power. As a cloak, the sect of Jews feigned pious religiosity, but inwardly these evil men were greedy lovers of Mammon who hated righteousness and gorged their vacuous souls on bloody violence and hatred of mankind. They were lovers of self, deniers of truth, killers of Christ.

Throughout the centuries, since the angry Jewish mob cried out to Pilate, *"Crucify him!,"* their wickedness in spirit has grown and matured in its viciousness and deceit. A particularly potent example of their grotesque nature and conduct is found in the decades that followed the October, 1917 overthrow of the Czar in Russia and the assumption to power of the Bolshevik communists.

Sixty-Six Million Innocents Perish

Jewish Freemasons Vladimir Lenin and Lev Bronstein (who deceptively called himself by the Russian surname, *Leon Trotsky*) and their fellow Jewish conspirators, with the financial aid of Jewish bankers (the Warburgs, Rothschilds, *et al*) and rabbis in the U.S. and Europe, transformed the Russian Empire into the greatest Orwellian system of monstrous genocide ever known. By the late 1930s, in a mere two decades, almost 50 million people, mostly Christians, had been brutalized and slaughtered.

By the 80s, the toll, according to historian Aleksandr Solzhenitsyn, had reached a staggering 66 million. Many perished in the communist's ruthlessly horrific gulag concentration camps. There were over 10,000 of these devilish centers of hell on earth.

Many of the commandants of these gulag camps were Jewish rabbis, and oh, how they enjoyed breaking the backs of miserable Christian prisoners, starving them, torturing them, freezing them, and finally, disposing of their wasted bodies by beating them to death with a billy club or putting a bullet through their brains.

Hatred Vented on Christians

The murderous Jewish thugs that banded together with Lenin, Trotsky and their thuggish cohort, Josef Stalin, vented all of their hatred on

Christians and Churches. The most beautiful of churches were burned to the ground, gutted out; some were turned into brothels, others into livestock and hog barns and pens. Pastors and priests were beaten, mocked, and herded like cattle into trucks and wagons and hauled away, never to be seen again. Entire congregations were destroyed.

After the Gold

Banks and businesses everywhere were robbed and plundered. Dentists' homes and offices were a special target. It was known that the dentists used gold and silver for tooth fillings. In a short time, nearly every dentist in the U.S.S.R. had been arrested and taken away as a "threat to the state" (what we in the U.S. today call "homeland security"). Their puny stores of silver and gold were confiscated, to be enjoyed by the new Jewish commissars.

The dentist shortage, as it turned out, backfired a wee bit. When Comrade Lenin came down one evening with a severe toothache, it seems there was not a single dentist left in all Moscow—each had been purged by the Cheka (security forces). Lenin raged at this oversight, but alas, it took three days to "extract" a lone dentist from a prison camp hundreds of miles distant where he languished for his alleged "crime" of being a member of the "rich bourgeoisie."

Sufferings and Terror Covered Up By Media

Now while all this mayhem, bloodshed, and carnage was going on, the western media and press were seemingly joyous at the ongoing Jewish Purim. Newspapers and magazines across America—most owned by Jews—celebrated with articles and editorials favorable to Lenin and his communist victors. Hundreds of thousands of Jews in the U.S. packed up their belongings and headed to Russia. They wanted to be part of the great victory and aid in setting up the world's first Zionist regime in the west. It would be the model for a global Jewish Utopia, founded on the principles of Judaism and the Talmud.

America's most famous rabbi at the time, Stephen Wise, proclaimed loudly, *"Judaism is Communism, and Communism is Judaism."*

The Anti-Semitism Act

Immediately after Lenin and his communist butchers had consolidated their power base, the new Peoples' Congress of the U.S.S.R. passed its

The Forward is the top Jewish publication in the United States. The building which houses this magazine has the heads of Marx and Engels, founders of Communism, carved in stone on its front piece. Gruesome reminders that the Jews were and are the main sponsors of Communism. As Rabbi Stephen Wise stated, *"Communism is Jewish."*

very first legislative bill, the *anti-Semitism Act*. The new law punished reported acts of "anti-Semitism" with the ultimate penalty: *Death*. The rabbis and their congregations danced in the aisles of their synagogues throughout the Soviet empire—and began to draw up lists of Gentiles (Goyim) whom they wanted the State to immediately prosecute for this new offense of anti-Semitism. Jews who turned in suspected anti-Semites were handsomely rewarded by the authorities.

An Unexpected Situation?

Now, we are told today that, like 9/11 and Pearl Harbor, no one could have seen coming what happened in Russian and its captive republics. President Woodrow Wilson, the British and French Prime Ministers, no one it is said, could ever have expected the *Red Terror* that ensued. Not even by the late 30s, when reports began to accumulate of the untold sorrow and tragedy that was occurring, was hardly a word echoed by the controlled, Jewish-owned press. Tens of millions suffered a cruel and pitiless fate while the world slept.

President Franklin D. Roosevelt even patterned his socialistic *New Deal* on the communist ideal. *The New York Times'* ace reporter, Walter Duranty, reported on-scene from Russia and sent back glowing reports. According to Duranty, economic and social miracles were being accomplished by the communist regime. *The New York Times* assured its readers that true democracy and freedom had become the order of the day in Soviet Russia, and that Lenin and Stalin were fast allies of America, a force for good in the world.

This propaganda lasted, in fact, until after World War II, when the truth began to force its way through, beginning with the reports from heroic General George Patton in Europe and flowering during the truth-filled days of the courageous and much despised Wisconsin Senator, Joseph McCarthy.

Finally, the everyday American and European knew of the untold horror that was Soviet Communism. However, what was not known is that Lenin and the others were Jews and that their bloody empire was instigated by Talmudic Zionist beasts intent on plundering the world through their unique blend of religion, greed, and hatred. I refer, of course, to Zio-Mammonism.

Sergius Nilus and His Prophetic Writings

But, amazingly, there was one solitary man who saw all this coming. His name: *Sergius Nilus*. Nilus was an humble Christian, an Orthodox priest, author, and—as it turned out—a prophet of God. In 1901, an astonishing manuscript came into his hands. It was entitled, *The Protocols of the Learned Elders of Zion*. Nilus got on his knees and begged God to tell him what to do with this hideous, but revealing, document, the Protocols.

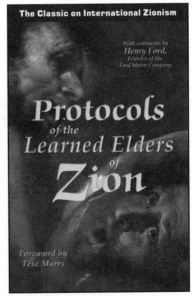

In 1905, Nilus published his prophetic book, *The Great Within the Small, and The Coming of Antichrist*. In this book, he prophesied that the country and people of Russia would soon undergo a terrible test. The antichrist spirit was about to be loosed. *The Protocols*, Nilus wrote, were the harbinger of this monumental evil soon to strike Russia, and also eventually engulf the whole world.

It would be the Zionist Jews—the Synagogue of Satan—destined to bring such grievous hardships in our midst. And their plot, warned Nilus, was meticulously documented in *The Protocols of the Learned Elders of*

Zion, which Nilus included as a section in his published book. The concluding passage from Nilus' book, *The Epilogue of Nilus*, is published below.

How incredible that only a dozen years later, in 1917, the Bolshevik Communists' grotesque crimes and atrocities began with the overthrow of Russia's monarchy.

A Plea to the Church

The heartbroken priest, Sergius Nilus, had seen it coming and had done his duty. He had faithfully published the Protocols. Moreover, in an epilogue in the book, he inserted a prophetic plea to the Church to heed the warning. It failed to do so.

Nilus soon became the target of the feared Cheka secret police. He was arrested. A communist judge angrily told Nilus that he was responsible for "incalculable damage" to the Soviet State. Nilus was sent to one of the worst of the prisons where he was tortured for his faith. Broken in body but not in spirit, after release from his

Sergius Nilus, Russian Christian monk and prophet who first published the *Protocols of the Learned Elders of Zion*. When the Jews seized power in Russia in 1917, Nilus was sent to prison.

prison cell—a miracle in itself—the tired and exhausted saint retired to a monastery where he lived as an outcast for his final three years, before being taken home to glory by the Lord Jesus.

Concluding Passage From the Epilogue of Nilus
By Sergius Nilus (1905)

According to the testament of Montefiore, Zion is not sparing, either of money or of any other means, to achieve its ends. In our day, all the governments of the entire world are consciously or unconsciously submissive to the commands of this great Supergovernment of Zion, because all the bonds and securities are in its hands; for all countries are indebted to the Jews for sums which they will never be able to pay. All affairs—industry, commerce, and diplomacy—are in the hands of Zion. It is by means of its capital loans that it has enslaved all nations. By keeping education on purely materialistic lines, the Jews have loaded the Gentiles with heavy chains with which they have harnessed them to their "Supergovernment."

The end of national liberty is near, therefore, personal freedom is approaching its close; for true liberty cannot exist where Zion uses the lever of its gold to rule the masses and dominate the most respectable and enlightened class of society.

"He that hath ears to hear, let him hear."

It is nearly four years since the Protocols of the Elders of Zion came into my possession. Only God knows what efforts I have made to bring them to general notice—in vain—and even to warn those in power, by disclosing the causes of the storm about to break on apathetic Russia who seems, in her misfortune, to have lost all notion of what is going on around her.

And it is only now when I fear it may be too late, that I have succeeded in publishing my work, hoping to put on their guard those who still have ears to hear and eyes to see. One can no longer doubt it, the triumphant reign of the King of Israel rises over our degenerate world as that of Satan, with his power and his terrors; the King born of the blood of Zion—the Antichrist—is about to mount the throne of universal empire.

Events are precipitated in the world at a terrifying speed: quarrels, wars, rumors, famines, epidemics, earthquakes—everything which even yesterday was impossible, today is an accomplished fact. One would think that the days pass so rapidly to advance the cause of the chosen people. Space does not allow us to enter into the details of world history with regard to the disclosed "mysteries of iniquity," to prove from history the influence which the "Wise Men of Zion" have exercised through universal misfortunes, by foretelling the certain and already near future of humanity, or by raising the curtain for the last act of the world's tragedy.

Only the light of Christ and of his Holy Church Universal can fathom the abyss of Satan and disclose the extent of its wickedness.

I feel in my heart that the hour has already struck when there should urgently be convoked an Eighth Ecumenical Council which would unite the pastors and representatives of all Christendom. Secular quarrels and schisms would all be forgotten in the imminent need of preparing against the coming of the Antichrist.

TWENTY

Refuting the Jewish Fable That Sustain Israel's War Against God and Man

Bloody Zion

Finally, a book that documents rebellious Israel and Judaism's long battle against God and against all of humanity. Edward Hendrie, in his new book, *Bloody Zion*, does exactly that. I thank God that He has, in Hendrie, raised up a man—a distinguished scholar and truth-teller to expose the Jewish fables that have long held many Christians and Christian churches in chains.

The Apostle Paul warned of the grave danger that befalls Christians who fall victim to Jewish lies—i.e. "fables" and man made myths. In his letter to *Titus (1:13-14)* we read:

> *"This witness is true. Wherefore rebuke them sharply, that they may be sound in faith; Not giving heed to Jewish fables, and commandments of men, that turn from the truth."*

I find it both grieving and distressing that so many today have become enmeshed in a dark cloud of Jewish fables. Mesmerized by their confused and errant pastors and by paid-off, bribed Zionist apologists, millions of deceived Christians and others have fallen prey to the "Jews are God's Chosen" fable, even though the Scriptures, in *Galatians 3:16-29* and Peter states clearly that it is those who are of Jesus who are the Chosen and spiritually are the True Israel of God. It is Christians, not believers in the corrupt religion of Judaism, who are *"Abraham's seed*

183

and heirs according to the promise."

Jews Guilty of Horrible Atrocities, Blood Crimes, and Monstrosities

Hendrie's new book, *Bloody Zion*, addresses these issues but it goes much further. The title of the book points to the massive evidence within its pages that since the days of physical Israel's Babylonian captivity and return, the Jews have been guilty and complicit in the most astonishing array of horrible atrocities, blood crimes, and monstrosities.

Filled with hatred toward God and man, the rabbis and their Zionist zealots have engaged in the most Luciferian of acts. True history exposes their founding of Illuminism and Communism. Hendrie even quotes the most famous of rabbis who have boasted that "Zionism is Communism."

Bloody Zion, by Edward Hendrie, documents the monstrous revolutionary activities of the Jewish nation and people throughout history. He proves the Babylonian origins of today's Judaism religion.

Jews Behind Satanic Movement Throughout History

Bloody Zion also illustrates how Zionist Jews are behind the darkness of Freemasonry and that virtually every satanic movement of the past 500 years began and sometimes thrived under the sponsorship and direction of revolutionary Jewish leaders.

No one can accurately gauge how many hundreds of millions of victims have fallen to instruments of torture and hideous death at the hands of these satanic Jews. The great Vatican Inquisition of Torquemada, the Jesuit conspiracies, the overthrow of Russia by the Bolsheviks, World War I and II—all these bloody events and more were the result of Jewish intrigue and diseased plots of the Zionists.

Today, fiery war has erupted as the Zionist neocons and apostate Christians are heard, applauding the bombs and bullets that Israel daily rains down on innocent, suffering, men, women, and children in Palestine.

Netanyahu has no sympathy for Arabs and other non-Jews and now has his mind set on destruction of Israel's ancient archenemies, Iran and Syria. Israel's Zionist warlords demand that America's military do the job of smashing Iran's teetering, embargoed economy and civilization.

In *Bloody Zion*, Hendrie unmasks the "Christian" leaders who support this death and destruction—The John Hagees, Billy Grahams, Pat Robertsons, *et al.* He shows how the powerful Jewish lobby in Washington, D. C. has given Israel's rabbinical coop a "License to Kill" and how the billionaire Jews who control our media and airwaves add to this mesmerizing cloud of deceit.

The Talmud Originated in Babylon

As for the pagan and racist religion of Judaism, *Bloody Zion* unmasks it's Talmudic teachings and doctrines, documenting their Babylonian origins. He writes, for example, that...

> "During the Babylonian captivity, an occult society of Jews
> replaced God's commands with Babylonian dogma. Their new
> religion became Judaism. Jesus explained the corruption of the
> Judaic religion: "Howbeit in vain do they worship me, teaching for
> doctrines the commandments of men" (Mark 7:7). Jesus revealed
> the satanic origin of Judaism when he stated: 'Ye are of your
> father the devil, and the lusts of your father ye will do' (John
> 8:44)."

"The Old Testament," Hendrie notes "documents the long history of rebellion against God." That unholy rebellion, he writes, "is defined by the crucifixion of Jesus Christ." But the Jews have never atoned for either their crimes against humanity, nor for their evil sin of murdering the Son of God. No, instead they relish their blood crimes and revel in their conquests and victories, all the while pretending that it is really they, the Jews, who have been the historical victim.

In their ages-old conspiracy, the Zionists have always sought to enforce a ban and censorship against any person who dares to document and point out the Jewish involvement in—indeed sponsorship of—bloody evil doing. By so doing, by shutting the mouths of the witnesses, the Zionists are convinced they can continue committing their potently wicked bloodletting.

Author of Bloody Zion

The book, *Bloody Zion*, will surely be hated by the Jewish power, here and abroad. Edward Hendrie will be reviled and despised and he can expect to be the target of smears and retribution.

But, from my personal discussions with Mr. Hendrie, I perceive that he is not a man to back down. Raised a hardcore Roman Catholic, educated in Catholic schools, a graduate of prestigious Notre Dame University and a Jesuit-run law school, Hendrie went on to become—and is today—an attorney of great renown. But most important, after all these personal achievements, Edward Hendrie one day met Jesus Christ and gave his heart, his soul, his life to Jesus and to Truth. That was what made the difference in his life, and it is what has since molded his character and tenacity.

You who have read Hendrie's earlier outstanding book, *Solving the Mystery of Babylon the Great*, know that Mr. Hendrie left the fold of Roman Catholicism and is now a Bible-believing Christian. In fact, *Solving the Mystery of Babylon the Great* effectively documents the Vatican connection with satanic Zionism and shows how that connection relates to the Bible's powerful last day's prophecies.

How many accomplished men or women do you know who are bold and brave enough to put their life and career on the line to ferret out the truth and then take on the two most powerful forces of evil on this planet—Jesuitic Catholicism and Zionist Judaism?

As long as we have courageous men like Edward Hendrie, inspired by God who stand up against the forces and historical tide of Zionist evil that sweeps this planet, we have hope. God always raises up a witness, lifting aloft the banner of truth.

You, dear friend, by your love of the truth and your support for *Power of Prophecy*, a truth-telling ministry, are demonstrating that you, too, are willing to serve as a witness. You, too, are bravely showing forth the banner of truth. That banner may become tattered. You, personally, may become a victim and be battered by the forces of evil who so desperately insist the truth be bottled up and cast away into the sea of forgetfulness. But be assured of this: The Truth will not fail. It cannot be simply swept away and dismissed. Jesus won a resounding victory for us on the cross some two thousand years ago. We, His disciples, carry on. The battle is at hand, but victory is ours. Of that, there is no doubt.

TWENTY-ONE

The Americans, the Russians, the British, and the French, fueled by satanic barbarism, brought torment and suffering to millions of innocents after World War II. It was better to be dead than alive in those days, when hell came down to earth.

Hellstorm

"And I heard a voice from heaven saying unto me, Write, Blessed are the dead which die in the Lord from henceforth: Yea, saith the Spirit, that they may rest from their labours; and their works do follow them."
— *Revelation 14:13*

You and I have often heard or read of it—the so-called "Good War" and its after-effects. World War II was a glorious time, say our textbooks. It was a time when an insane, juvenile and clownish imbecile, Adolf Hitler, and his storm troopers rampaged across Europe and Russia. Hitler built concentration camps, and he and the Nazis did terrible things to innocent people. They murdered six-million Jews in a monstrous holocaust.

The masters of Hollywood tell us it was the wonderful, compassionate, caring troops of the American military, helped by dedicated Soviet, British, and French allies, who eventually ended the great conflict. Yes, the great generals Ike, Bradley, Montgomery and others deserve the credit. They took the evil Nazis by the nape of their necks, forced them

187

to be tried at Nuremberg and elsewhere for their terrible crimes, and severely punished the guilty. All the Nazi leaders—Hitler, Goering, Himmler, *et al*, were executed or committed suicide.

The Story Goes

The story goes that, justice done, the victors then took upon themselves the heroic task of rebuilding the stricken German nation. It was our food, our fuel, our hard work, our organization, our personnel that saved the day. Oh, how magnificent were these paragons of goodness. Christ Jesus Himself must have supervised their work.

In no time at all, the factories in Germany were humming again; the weapons of war destroyed, democracy installed. The citizens of Germany were gleaming with pride and happiness.

The Germans, you see, owed their remarkable recovery, their very existence, to the victors. We had saved them from the clutches of their Nazi overlords. We had restored righteousness, we had rescued the masses. *All hail the marvelous overcomers of evil Nazi Germany.*

Hollywood movies, of course, have aided in building our memories. The official government account has also been recounted in thousands of books, all published by establishment publishing houses. These sources paint the oft-told account that lodges in our heads. It's goody-goody Franklin D. Roosevelt, America, and the U.S.S.R. against the wicked, immoral, monstrous Nazis. Yes, this is what we have been told.

But, What is the Truth?

But, Sir Winston Churchill, allied leader and victor, mysteriously, once said, *"The truth must be accompanied by a bodyguard of lies."*

What did Churchill mean?

That astute writer, George Orwell, also said, *"Telling the truth is a revolutionary act."*

What, exactly, was he talking about?

Is the story told us of World War II and the years afterward of the "miraculous" German recovery aided by the Allies basically just a bunch of *lies*? To get at the truth, will it be necessary for you and I to become a *revolutionary* truthteller?

The Truth Comes Out—Painfully and Slowly

Well, now, almost 75 years after the official end to World War II, the truth

Red Army soldiers hoist the Soviet flag over Berlin in 1945. Then began the rapes, pillaging, and atrocities of the Jews who ruled over East Germany.

has emerged: slowly; painfully; sadly. The truth that has been covered up by censorship, mass propaganda and by truth embargo imposed by the Jewish-owned press and establishment in America.

It is, straightly put, the *internet* and a few courageous researchers that has made it possible for the truth to rise up from the mist and stench of the official swamp. Only the internet is free, and the establishment is desperate to shackle it. Soon, it, too, will be closed.

Those who now tell the truth—about the World Wars, about Vietnam, about Judaism, about the Federal Reserve, and thousands of other "propaganda achievements" are the enemy of the monied few. They are hated and despised because they love and embrace the truth. Therefore, the purveyors of falsehoods hate and despise *you* and *me*.

Now, let me go straight to the subject at hand—the so-called "victory" over Germany and the much ballyhooed "miraculous recovery" of that nation. Many new, truthful books are now coming out. We now know of the horrors, and fateful crimes perpetrated by our leaders against the defeated men, women, and children of Germany.

Annihilation by ground and air was not enough. *Mass murder, rape, plunder, torture, beatings, starvation were all employed.* These brutal tactics lasted years after the official end of hostilities. Millions of innocent and unsuspecting German citizens were roughly herded into allied concentration camps, in places like Zuffenhausen, Worms, Langwasser, Bretzenheim and Bad Nenndorf. There they were beaten, tortured, starved, frozen, and otherwise killed.

They were little fed, except for feces-filled, watery "soup." Given little or no shelter, untold thousands froze to death.

Meanwhile, their conquerors—Americans, British, Russians— enjoyed abundant foodstuffs, and fuel was plentiful.

Any prisoner bold enough to complain was taken out and executed. Daily, scores of the dead were gathered and burned in mass pits. This is how and where the so-called *"holocaust tales and pictures"* come from.

Germany's economy was intentionally destroyed after the war's conclusion. As Keeling writes, in *Gruesome Harvest*, the allies sought "the permanent destruction of Germany's industrial heartland." This caused, he notes, such *"consequences as the death through starvation and disease of millions and tens of millions of Germans."*

A Demonic Jewish Blueprint, the Morgenthau Plan

Were these torturous deaths the unavoidable result of war? No, it was not. This was *planned death*, caused by Truman's approval of the demonic Jewish blueprint, the *Morgenthau Plan*. Morgenthau was a Jew high-up in the Truman administration who led the *Manhattan Cabal* of wealthy Jews dedicated to promoting world *Zionism*. It was this cabal that, in 1933, had begun a great world war against the Nazis.

The *Morgenthau Plan* was their war revenge. Devised by a sick, pathological Jew, it was incorporated into clause 6 of the Joint Chiefs of Staff Order 1067.

One can read more about the *Morgenthau Plan* in the incredible book—suppressed for 70 years but finally released—written by none other than former President Herbert Hoover, titled *Freedom Betrayed— Herbert Hoover's Secret History of the Second World War and Its Aftermath*, and published by Stanford University Press.

Here are more scholarly, documented books, belatedly published, that also give us unvarnished facts:

• *Revisiting the Good War's Aftermath: Emerging Truths in an Ocean*

TIME
The Weekly Newsmagazine

SECRETARY OF THE TREASURY

Volume XXIV   Number 12

Time magazine had this cover in 1934 showing Roosevelt's Secretary of the Treasury, Henry Morgenthau. *The Morgenthau Plan*, implemented in Germany after the allied victory, resulted in millions of innocent Germans being intentionally killed. When he became President, Harry Truman recognized that Morgenthau was insane and fired him.

of Myths, by Dwight Murphy, Wichita State University Press

• *After the Reich: The Brutal History of the Allied Occupation,* by Giles MacDonough, Basic Books

• *Gruesome Harvest: The Allies Postwar War Against the German People,* by Ralph Franklin Keeling, Institute for Historical Review

• *Other Losses—An Investigation into the Mass Deaths of German Prisoners at the Hands of the French and Americans After World War II*, by James Bacque, Toronto: Stoddard Publishing Co.

• *Red Storm on the Reich—The Soviet March on Germany*, by Christopher Duffy, Atheneon Press

• *The Destruction of Dresden*, by David Irving, London: Wm. Kimler & Co.

Hellstorm: The Death of Nazi Germany 1944-1947

Each of these books provide gruesome, truthful details on what it was like to have been an unarmed, noncombatant German in the immediate years after World War II. One of the best books I have come upon is *Hellstorm: The Death of Nazi Germany, 1944-1947,* by Thomas Goodrich. I have also interviewed Mr. Goodrich on *Power of Prophecy* radio.

Goodrich's book is so vivid that one can almost smell the putrid odor of decaying bodies through its pages. In a letter to me, Goodrich wrote that he is so sick and alarmed over his research, that he intends to spend the rest of his life exposing the horrors of what occurred.

I invite you, my dear friends, to order and read this exceptional book. You will be glad you did, for the truth is always powerful and liberating. Here, below, is a synopsis of *Hellstorm.*

~~~~~~~~~~~~~~~~~~~~~~~~~~~

Demons Danced in Satanic Glee while the Soldiers Raped, Robbed, and Murdered

It was the worst of days. The war was over, but not the carnage. In town after town, in village after village, whether in mansions or in farmhouses, the assaults and murders of unarmed civilians continued. Mothers, grandmothers, little girls—age made no difference. Fathers and brothers had their throats slit. Homes were vandalized—pillaged, then burned to the ground. And the women were cruelly raped, some 30 or even 100 times, each. Then, mercifully, many were strangled and bludgeoned to death. It was better to be dead than alive, in those days.

This is the true story of Germany, home of the legendary Hansel and Gretel, but after being victimized and brought down to hell by the Soviet hordes and the American adventurers, a place of great sorrow. A place of unparalleled blood and suffering.

In the western part of Germany, millions of defeated soldiers—some as young as 13 and 14—were cramped behind barbed wire, without shelter, pounded by the cold and bitter rain, with only a bit of gruel for food. They had believed their captors, the Americans, would be compassionate. They were wrong. Millions perished. The few survivors of these horrendous concentration camps only wished they, too, were dead.

The broken cities, meanwhile, were in ruins and ashes, unnecessarily burnt and bombed to the ground. Few had food, rarely even a few potatoes. Poor little crying children begged mothers for a crumb of bread. At night, the survivors made fires and shivered together outside in the deep cold.

A German city fire bombed by allied bomber aircraft. Most surviving German women were unmercifully raped and beaten.

This was when hell came down to earth—a savage period that is the darkest and best-kept secret in the history of mankind. Now, more than 70 years later, Tom Goodrich in his breathtaking book, *Hellstorm* reveals the horror of those monstrous days of Germany, 1944-1947. Why have these monumental crimes been covered up for so long? And why do they still attempt to keep it from you and me?

~~~~~~~~~~~~~~~~~~~~~~~~~~

The Fantastic Words of Jesus Christ

But do keep one thing in perspective. It is not the fighting men of America who are responsible for these heinous and irresponsible crimes against humanity. They were and are among its victims. It is our leaders, communist and Jews in the Roosevelt Administration—lying, rotten, corrupt, scheming and vicious.

In fact, the men responsible for these awful crimes also are guilty of the murder of two great men who attempted to unmask these horrors: General George Patton and Secretary of Defense James Forrestal. I will have more to say about their mysterious murders in future books, God willing. Until then, remember these fantastic words of our Lord and Saviour, Jesus Christ:

"Ye shall know the truth, and the truth shall make you free."
                — *Jesus Christ*

TWENTY-TWO

Why Do Jews Show No Guilt or Remorse Over Their Heartless Murder of Christ Jesus?

Remorseless Killers of Zion

"We killed Jesus, and we're proud of it."
— Jewish Youth, on *YouTube*

S ome 2,000 years ago, the Sanhedrin, made up of the high priests of Judaism, ordered the killing of Christ Jesus. The Jews' holy book, the Babylonian Talmud, brags about the killing of Jesus. The Jews make it known that it was not the Romans, but a proper rabbinical court that ordered his death, and it was well deserved. Here are but a few actual quotes from their Talmud:

Sanhedrin, 67a: Jesus was hanged on the eve of Passover.

Sanhedrin, 103a and *1076:* Jesus was adjudged guilty of seducing, corrupting, and attempting to destroy Israel.

Zohar III, 282: Jesus died like a beast and was buried in an animal's dirt heap.

Gittin, 57a: Jesus was punished by being sent to hell and being boiled in hot, fiery excrement.

195

So this is what the Jews, in their most holy book, the Talmud, say about Jesus Christ. And every word in the Talmud is honored by the rabbis as "Divine Truth."

Rabbi Michael Radkinson, one of today's greatest authorities on Jewish holy books, in his *The History of the Talmud*, states:

> "The Talmud is one of the wonders of the world. Not a single letter of it is missing. It still dominates the minds of a whole people (the Jews) who venerate its contents as Divine Truth."

Jewish Youth Are Proud of Killing Jesus

In a *YouTube* video, I recently witnessed two young Jewish thugs terrorizing a Palestinian family. They demanded, *"Get out of Israel. This is our land. God gave it to us."*

When the Palestinians protested, explaining they were *"Christian believers,"* the two Jewish thugs really grew angry. One shouted, *"F..k your Jesus! We killed Jesus, and we're proud of it."*

Jewish comics are dominant at the casinos in Las Vegas and on television. They get big laughter making fun of Jesus death and deriding Christianity. Here is Sarah Silverman in her communist red T-shirt with its Soviet star and in yet another pose.

These two young Jews showed their hatred toward Jesus. I have never, ever heard one Jew say that he or she is sorry that his ancestors killed Jesus. Most brag openly that they'd do it again.

Sarah Silverman, Jewish comedian, stated on her HBO-TV special, that she'd do it right this time: *"I'd put his body in a meat grinder and make mincemeat of it,"* she said. *"Presto! No more Jesus!"*

Her live audience roared with laughter.

Jews Offer No Apology for Killing Jesus

We live in an age of apology and confession. Everyone seems to be confessing what they or their ancestors did wrong and apologizing for it. The Pope has apologized to the Jews for the Catholic Church having persecuted them in past history. The Germans paid—and still pay—billions in reparations to alleged holocaust victims. Whites who practiced apartheid in South Africa apologized and made black Nelson Mandela head of their country. In the U.S.A., our Congress apologized to the blacks for the wrong done them in slavery.

Young Jews taunt a Palestinian woman in Israel. This is common behavior and often ends in the victim being beaten. This defenseless woman had her clothes torn off by the thugs.

But the Jews have *never* apologized to *anyone*, especially to the Christians for having killed Jesus. In fact, the Jews believe themselves to be perfect "God-men." They never apologize to anyone. We know, of course, of the horrific crimes of the Jews during the French Revolution. Later, in the 20th century, the Jews in Soviet Russia were responsible for the purging and murder of 66,000,000 hapless innocents.

However, to this day, though the Jews harp incessantly about the wrong done them by Hitler and the Nazis in supposedly putting some *six million* to death, they never utter one word of apology or regret for their tribe massacring eleven times that many in the U.S.S.R.

Why is this? Why do the Jews obstinately refuse to apologize for their countless crimes against humanity? Why do they brag and even laugh about their dishonorable killing of Jesus? Why do the Jews display such a monumental lack of remorse?

I know the answer to this question. It is because most Jews are *psychopaths*.

Psychopaths Feel No Remorse

Professor Robert Hare, a criminal psychologist, is the world's leading expert on criminal psychopaths. "It stuns me, as much as it did 40 years ago when I started, that it is possible to have people so emotionally disconnected that they can function as if other people are objects to be manipulated and destroyed without any concern," Hare says.

Hare has developed a test of 20 criteria to determine if a person (or possibly an entire nation or race) is of a psychopathic mind. Amazingly, the Jews possess every single one of these deviant traits. For example, they possess glibness and superficial charm and have a grandiose sense of self-worth. The psychopath is a pathological liar; he is cunning and manipulative, emotionally shallow, callous and lacking in empathy, unwilling to accept responsibility, has a parasitic lifestyle and, most of all, lacks remorse.

Today, our criminal justice system in most states allows the family of convicted murderers to stand up at the conclusion of a trial, and tell the convicted person of the pain he has caused by taking the life of their loved one.

It has always seemed to me that this is a ridiculous thing because the cries of anguish of the victims' families, does not at all cause the callous murderer to feel empathy. He has no remorse, and so all the time the family member spends pouring out his heart is wasted. The murderer sits passively and rarely shows any feelings. If he does, it's all a big show, designed to fool and deceive the Judge into giving him a lighter sentence.

Psychopaths Are Not Like You and Me

The Jew, particularly, doesn't waste his breath on the Christian who confronts him with his crime. The Talmud is a book the Christian never reads, so the Jew simply sits back and refuses to take responsibility. *"Jesus was responsible for his own death,"* the Jew will explain. Or, *"Hey, the Roman soldiers carried out his crucifixion. It wasn't the Jews."*

When someone like actor/director Mel Gibson produces a movie *(The Passion of the Christ)* fingering the Jews, the Jewish ADL and other Jews become hysterical. They scream and shout, *"anti-Semite!"*

Here again, this is a definite sign of the tainted psychopath mind. A criminal is always likely to blame the victim, remarking "He shouldn't

Having no sympathy at all for his suffering and no guilt for his crucifixion, the Jews screamed "anti-Semite" at director Mel Gibson for his accurate depiction of the brutality rendered Christ in the movie, *The Passion of the Christ.*

have got in the way," or "That girl shouldn't have dressed like that. She was asking for it," or something similar.

Psychopaths are not like you and me, says Professor Hare and other authorities. They have no remorse. They're glad they murdered or raped. They will do it again given the chance. They are truly like aliens from another galaxy in their thinking. To expect them to understand the pain and despair they inflict on others is not reasonable. They are immoral, lacking in empathy devoid of human feelings.

The Jewish Psychopath Cannot Reform

Dr. Hare says that, regrettably, the psychopath cannot reform. We can't make him feel for his victims or have remorse at what he has done. He is what he is.

Jesus put it this way in *Matthew 24*, when he flatly told the Jews: *"You are of your father the devil, and his works you will do."* A psychopath is, in fact, a devil in human form.

Only Jesus Himself can change or redeem the psychopath. But few will receive Him into their heart. No remorse, no regret, remember?

The Apostle Paul said that the Jews *"killed the Lord Jesus, and their own prophets... and are contrary to all men"* (I Thes. 2:15).

Isn't it, therefore, insane of the Christian Zionists to exalt and praise the very ones, the psychopaths, the devil men, who not only killed the Saviour, Jesus Christ, but also killed their own prophets? These deceived Christian Zionists are so full of demonic spirit that, in defiance of the Bible's clear teaching, they actually lift up and praise the psychopath Jews and exalt them as *"God's Chosen People."* May Jesus forgive them for this horrible, satanic doctrine.

"Wherefore he saith, awake thou that sleepest, and arise from the dead, and Christ shall give thee light." (Ephesians 5:14)

TWENTY-THREE

As Jewish "Proselytes," the Khazars are...

Twofold More the Child of Hell

"Woe unto you, scribes and pharisees, hypocrites! For ye compass sea and land to make one proselyte, and when he is made, ye make him twofold more the child of hell than yourselves."

— Jesus Christ
Matthew 23:15

"Most Jews do not like to admit it, but our God is Lucifer... We are his chosen people..."

— Harold Rosenthal
The Hidden Tyranny (1970)

Every person who truthfully speaks of the evil works of the Jews finds themselves very quickly being angrily criticized by Zionist know-nothings. The Judaizers who believe themselves "Christians" are the worst. They actually believe that if a person says even one negative word about Jews, he or she will be severely punished by Jesus on Judgment Day.

Not one of these know-nothings has apparently read the Holy Bible. If they did, they would find plenty of folks who have blasted the Jews and exposed their evildoing. Here are just a few of the many who say bad, bad things about the Jews: Moses, Jeremiah, Isaiah, Hosea, Ezekiel, Elijah, Amos, Stephen, Peter, Paul, and John. Shall I go on?

Indeed, all of the prophets and apostles were harshly critical of the Jews, their sin and their wickedness. Most were, in turn, viciously attacked by the reprobate Jews and some were unjustly punished with death because they upheld God's standards and exposed the rabbis, priests and other evildoers.

Now, should all of these great men have kept their mouths shut? What of the modern-day "Christians"—who explode with self-righteousness when Jews are criticized?

Do you see how ridiculous these make-believe "Christians" are? Who taught them such silliness? Their pastors and ministers?

Jesus: #1 Critic of Jews in the Bible

In fact, it could just be that the #1 critic of the Jews in all the Bible was—now, get ready for it, true Christians—*Jesus Christ Our Lord!*

Jesus did not spare the Jews. He said the most poignant, yet truthful, things right to their face. Jesus was not shy about what he thought. He told the Jews: "Ye are as graves which appear not, and the men that walk over them are not aware of them" *(Luke 11:44)*.

Jesus said unto the Jews, "Woe unto you! For ye build the sepulchers (gravesites) of the prophets, and your fathers killed them. Truly ye bear witness that ye allow the deeds of your fathers" *(Luke 11:43-48)*. Jesus prophesied there would be more martyrs to come.

> *"I will send them prophets and apostles, and some of them they shall slay and prosecute. That the blood of all the prophets, which was shed from the foundation of the world, may be required of this generation." (Luke 11:49-50)*

Jesus lambasted the Jews, proclaiming "O generation of vipers, how can ye, being evil, speak good things?" *(Matthew 12:34)*

"The Son of man," warned Jesus, "shall send forth his angels, and they shall gather out of his kingdom all things which offend, and them which do iniquity; And shall cast them into a furnace of fire: there shall be wailing and gnashing of teeth" *(Matthew 13: 41-42)*.

Jesus Took Away the Kingdom From the Jews

Using direct words that no wicked Jew could misunderstand, Jesus went on to declare:

> *"Therefore, say I unto you, the kingdom of God shall be taken from you, and given to a nation bringing forth the fruits thereof." (Matthew 21:43)*

Why did Jesus take the kingdom from the Jews? Because of the blackness and evil in their hearts. Clearly, the Jews were not of God but of Satan, and Jesus told them exactly who was their father:

> *"Ye are of your father the devil, and the lusts of your father ye will do..." (John 8:44)*

Could the very Christ, Jesus our Saviour, have chosen more harsh and critical words to describe the evil Jews? Are you not ashamed, Judaizer "Christian," when a man of God today, seeking to follow Jesus' example, tells the world the obvious truth about the wickedness of the Jews? And you, hypocrite, attempt to divert the righteous by bludgeoning him with your untoward and wicked words. I say to you Judaizers: *Shut your mouth, lest God be offended rightly by your pretense and coverup!*

Khazar Jews: "Twofold More the Child of Hell"

Those who today speak the truth about Israel and the Jews should be commended by their fellow Christians. As proven in my book, *DNA Science and the Jewish Bloodline*, the Jews of Israel, the U.S.A., and Europe are not even Israelites. They are converts to Judaism from Khazaria, provinces in the Caucasus, in Southern Russia. As such, the Khazars—who comprise some 95 percent of *all* the "Jews" in the world—are even more wicked and depraved than those who schooled them on Judaism. It was, in fact, the Babylonian rabbis who, in the 8th century, taught the Khazars the Luciferian doctrines of the Talmud and Kabbalah.

As DNA science proves, the Khazars are *not* the seed of Abraham but are *pretenders* who masquerade as blood Jews. They are the Synagogue of Satan, whom Jesus said would blaspheme His name and persecute the true people of God:

"I know the blasphemy of them which say they are Jews, and are not,
but are the synagogue of Satan." (Revelation 2:9)

The Khazars are "proselytes" of the Jewish rabbis who, invited into Khazaria by King Bulan, eagerly came from nearby Babylon where they had been in exile these many years. They proceeded then to teach their new proselytes, the Khazars, of all the wickedness and Luciferian thought contained in that most hideous of religious textbooks, the Babylonian Talmud and the occultic Kabbalah.

In so doing, the rabbis fulfilled the very prophecy of Jesus Christ Himself, who straitlaced the satanic Jews, declaring:

"Woe unto you, scribes and pharisees, hypocrites! For ye compass
sea and land to make one proselyte, and when he is made, ye make
him two-fold more the child of hell than yourselves." (Matthew 23:15)

Khazars are Spiritually "Jews" by Their Own Admission

The Khazars have taken upon themselves the burden of their Jewish teachers, even falsely claiming that they, the Khazars, are of the some bloodline as the Jews. Very well, then, Khazars, you are what your mouths say you are. You are the *Synagogue of Satan*, twofold more the child of hell as were your predecessors.

By your own proud words and will, you demand to be known not as Khazars but as "Jews."

And so shall you be. "Wherefore ye be witnesses unto yourselves, that ye are the children of them which killed the prophets."

"Fill ye up then the measure of your fathers. Ye serpents, ye
generation of vipers, how can ye escape the damnation of hell."
(Matthew 23:31-33)

If you had not known of the grave crimes your Jewish spiritual Fathers had committed, you would be innocent. But you know, and you obscenely revel in that wicked knowledge. You, Jesus said, are serpents, two-fold the children of the devil. *How then, can you escape the damnation of hell?*

INDEX

ABOUT THE AUTHOR

Well-known author of the #1 national bestseller, *Dark Secrets of The New Age*, Texe Marrs has written books for such major publishers as Simon & Schuster, John Wiley, Prentice Hall/Arco, McGraw-Hill, and Dow Jones-Irwin. His books have sold millions of copies. He is one of the world's foremost symbologists and is a first-rate scholar of ancient history and Mystery religions.

Texe Marrs was assistant professor of aerospace studies, teaching American defense policy, strategic weapons systems, and related subjects at the University of Texas at Austin for five years. He has also taught international affairs, political science, and psychology for two other universities. A graduate *summa cum laude* from Park College, Kansas City, Missouri, he earned his Master's degree at North Carolina State University.

As a career USAF officer (now retired), he commanded communications-electronics and engineering units. He holds a number of military decorations including the Vietnam Service Medal and Presidential Unit Citation, and has served in Germany, Italy, and throughout Asia.

President of RiverCrest Publishing in Austin, Texas, Texe Marrs is a frequent guest on radio and TV talk shows throughout the U.S.A. and Canada. His monthly newsletter, *Power of Prophecy*, is distributed around the world, and he is heard globally on his popular, international shortwave and internet radio program, *Power of Prophecy*. His articles and research are published regularly on his exclusive websites: *powerofprophecy.com* and *conspiracyworld.com*.

FOR OUR NEWSLETTER

Texe Marrs offers a free sample copy of his newsletter focusing on world events, false religion, and secret societies, cults, and the occult challenge to Christianity. If you would like to receive this newsletter, please write to:

Power of Prophecy
1708 Patterson Road
Austin, Texas 78733

You may also e-mail your request to:
customerservice1@powerofprophecy.com

FOR OUR WEBSITE

Texe Marrs' newsletter is published free monthly on our website. This website has descriptions of all Texe Marrs' books, and are packed with interesting, insight-filled articles, videos, breaking news, and other information. You also have the opportunity to order an exciting array of books, tapes, and videos through our online Catalog and Sales Stores. Visit our website at:

www.powerofprophecy.com

OUR RADIO PROGRAMS

Texe Marrs' international radio program, *Power of Prophecy*, is broadcast weekly on shortwave radio throughout the United States and the world. *Power of Prophecy* can be heard on WWCR at 4.840 Sunday nights at 9:00 p.m. Central Time. You may also listen to *Power of Prophecy* 24/7 on website *www.powerofprophecy.com*.

Texe Marrs is also pastor and host of *Bible Home Church*. You may listen to Bible Home Church 24/7 on website *www.biblehomechurch.org*.

MORE RESOURCES FOR YOU

Books:

(For all orders, please include shipping and handling charge)

Bloody Zion—Refuting the Jewish Fables That Sustain Israel's War Against God and Man, by Edward Hendrie (544 pages) $28.00

Conspiracy of the Six-Pointed Star—Eye Opening Revelations and Forbidden Knowledge About Israel, the Jews, Zionism, and the Rothschilds, by Texe Marrs (432 pages) $25.00

Codex Magica—Secret Signs, Mysterious Symbols, and Hidden Codes of the Illuminati, by Texe Marrs (624 pages) $35.00

Conspiracy World—A Truthteller's Compendium of Eye-Opening Revelations and Forbidden Knowledge, by Texe Marrs (432 pages) $25.00

DNA Science and the Jewish Bloodline, by Texe Marrs (256 pages) $20.00

Gods of the Lodge, by Reginald Haupt (195 pages) $15.00

Judaism's Strange Gods, by Michael Hoffman (381 pages) $22.00

Matrix of Gog—From the Land of Magog Came the Khazars to Destroy and Plunder, by Daniel Patrick (160 pages) $18.00

Mysterious Monuments—Encyclopedia of Secret Illuminati Designs, Masonic Architecture, and Occult Places, by Texe Marrs (624 pages) $35.00

New Age Cults and Religions, by Texe Marrs (354 pages) $20.00

On the Jews and Their Lies, by Martin Luther (240 pages) $20.00

Protocols of the Learned Elders of Zion (320 Pages) $20.00

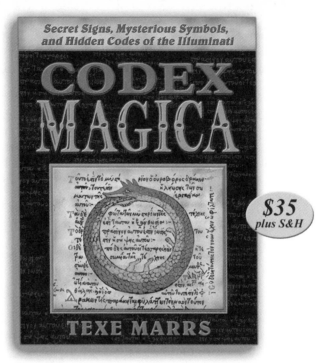

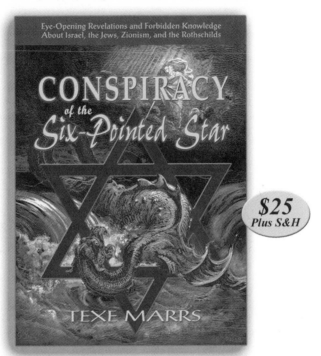

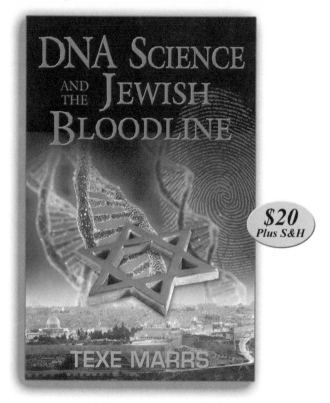